# aRt
## of
# Layers

Ronda Palazzari

simple * Techniques

* inVentive Scrapbook Pages

imagiNative * Papercrafts

NORTH
LIGHT
BOOKS

Cincinnati, Ohio
CreateMixedMedia.com

# contents

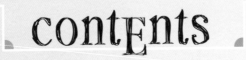

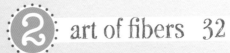

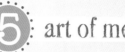

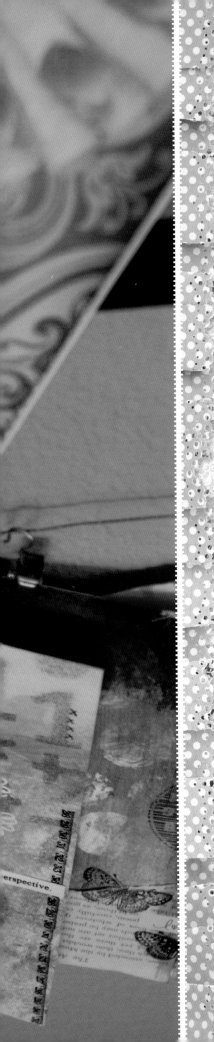

Trying new techniques and playing in my studio makes me giddy with excitement. With **Art of Layers**, my hope is that you become excited (and giddy) learning all these tips and tricks and then begin to play. You can combine two or three techniques, layering them together, and experimenting, to add so much interest and beauty to any project. Nothing makes me happier than building layers of art on my scrapbook pages, seeing patterned paper layered on top of old book prints, or on painted scraps, and then adding in the perfect embellishment for the completed look. To build up each layer until the page or piece of art is complete is just heavenly.

The journey in creating and layering is just as important and enjoyable as the final project. So get messy, start playing around, inventing, dissecting, and most importantly—have fun!

*Layer and Play*

i Dedicate tHis book to

My husband, Andrew, and our beautiful children, Lexi and Anthony. Thank you for your constant support and love, you make my life beautiful.

To Chrissi, (a.k.a. Kiki, Kooker, and my favorite nickname, Mule). I love you and miss you every single day. Love, Nag.

# 1

art of pAper

People often ask, "If you only could have a couple of items when scrapbooking or making art, which would you choose?" Paper and scissors—absolutely. I love patterned paper and always have a stock of it in my studio. I love the variety in the designs and colors of paper. There is an anticipation that I enjoy before seeing the newly released patterned papers, while still treasuring the good, classic patterns that have been around for years. It may have been the design or theme, but I used to be afraid of some patterned papers and found them too overwhelming to work with. Now I look at paper and all I can see are the possibilities. Paper can be a background, a mat for a photo, strips to accent a page, a border or even an embellishment. When you decide how to make the papers work for you, they are no longer overwhelming.

Throughout this chapter, I will show you how to manipulate cardstock, patterned papers and transparencies to create beautiful papercrafts and scrapbook layouts. Starting with the basics of layering patterned papers, we will dig deeper, making our own embossed cardstock paper, flower embellishments and paper lace. Finally, we will turn transparency paper into cool shapes that provide the perfect accents to any page or papercraft.

# patterned paper

I love using patterned paper to create layers on my layouts. This simple technique is great because you can add so many different textures to your layouts or papercrafts, and tearing the edges of the patterned papers integrates even more texture into a layout. So grab your favorite patterned papers and get ready to create drama in your pages with just a few pieces!

## THE PUSH & PULL

The story behind this layout came from a trying day as a parent of a teenage daughter. The push-and-pull theme is carried through on this layout with the contrast of a black-and-white photo next to a color one, the dictionary pages with the definitions of "young lady" and "adult" showing, plus the cameos of a young girl and a woman placed back to back.

I knew that I had more journaling than I could fit in one little section on the page, so I decided to use hidden journaling, but I wanted it to be obvious that there was more to the story than just the title. The tags I decided to use just scream "Pull me!" and reinforce the overall push-and-pull theme. I also added little numbers to the tags to impose some order on the text.

Supplies: alphabet stickers (American Crafts, Jenni Bowlin); patterned paper (Hambly Screenprints, Jenni Bowlin, October Afternoon); ink (Jenni Bowlin); chipboard buttons (Lily Bee Designs); transparency (Hambly Screenprints); paint (Ranger Industries); embroidery floss (DMC); tickets (Pink Paislee); twine (The Twinery); pen (Sakura Color Products); tags (Staples); other: dictionary pages

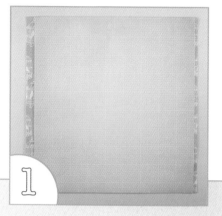

Materials: neutral patterned paper, grid or ledger patterned paper, paper trimmer, small-print patterned paper, paper piercer

1 Start with a neutral patterned paper as the background. Using a paper trimmer, trim a piece of grid or ledger patterned paper to 11½" (29cm) wide. Layer the grid or ledger paper off-center on top of the neutral background.

## layered with love

Try using smaller pieces in a focused area to create excitement on your pages. Use those beautiful scraps of patterned paper you have leftover to layer. Mix up large-print patterned paper with small-print patterned paper. Roll, rip, punch or sand the edges to give them a touch of dimension.

2 Cut a piece of small-print patterned paper to 10½" (27cm) wide. Rip the small-print patterned paper along the left side, pulling the edge towards the front so the torn, white edge will show clearly.

3 Roll the ripped edge of the small-print patterned paper to create a curled edge. Using a thin, rounded object, like the barrel of a paper piercer, makes this step easier.

4 Place the small-print patterned paper on the grid patterned paper, again off-center.

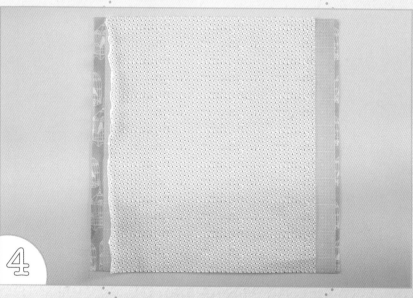

# quilted paper shapes

I always end up with little scraps of patterned paper that I cannot bear to just throw into the recycling bin. They are too pretty! Just like a patch-work quilt, this technique is perfect for using up those scraps you love.

## HER FUNNY GUY

When we lost my sister Chrissi, my son Anthony wasn't sure how to express his emotions. I knew it was important to document their bond of laughter because I wanted him to remember how he touched her life with his gift of quick-witted humor. After seeing this layout and these pictures, he is willing to talk about things more and even asked me to print one of these pictures for his wallet.

Supplies: alphabet (Studio Calico); bling (Me & My Big Ideas); cardstock (American Crafts); embossing powder, ink (Ranger Industries); patterned paper (Lily Bee Designs, Crate Paper, The Girls' Paperie); pen (Sakura Identi Pen); spray ink (Maya Road); stamps (Purple Onion Designs)

## HOT SUMMER DAYS **TAG**

The patchwork paper can take on many looks. On this particular tag, I used the same sized strips of patterned paper on the cardstock and then cut out my kite shape. Instead of stitching between the pieces of patterned paper, I covered the kites with clear embossing powder and outlined them with a black pen.

Supplies: cardstock (American Crafts); clear embossing powder, ink (Ranger Industries); fabric strips, patterned paper (Studio Calico); fabric tissue (Butterick); patterned paper (BasicGrey, Glitz Designs, Jillibean Soup, October Afternoon); pen (Sakura Identi Pen); sticker (October Afternoon); twine (The Twinery); other: fabric, dictionary pages

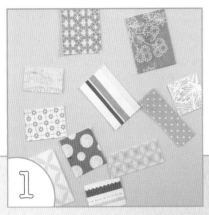

Materials: scraps of patterned paper, scissors, cardstock, glue stick, sewing machine and thread, pencil, Cloud Shape template* (optional), black pen

*Cloud Shape template on page 122.

1 Cut scraps of patterned paper into small strips and squares.

2 Adhere the strips and squares randomly to a plain piece of cardstock using a glue stick. Mix bold patterns with small-scale patterns to fill the page.

3 Machine stitch with a zigzag stitch anywhere the patterned paper edges meet.

4 Use a pencil to draw the cloud shape onto the quilted paper. You can draw the cloud freehand, or you can use the Cloud Shape template on page 122 if you prefer.

5 Cut out the cloud shape. Machine stitch with a straight stitch along the inside edge of the cloud shape.

6 Outline the outside edge of the cloud with a black pen.

## shape it up

Try to choose your favorite shapes to complement your story, like I did choosing a cloud. You can create a whole page using those fabulous scraps and then cut out shapes using templates, stencils, or drawing an image freehand. Try using some embroidery stitches between your piece of paper or embossing over the whole image to add different textures.

# hand-cut details

I am always looking for smaller details in those patterned papers that are begging to stand out. There are obvious ones, like flowers, and then there are diamonds in the rough waiting to be discovered.

## NOT SO TYPICAL

When Andy and I were engaged, we couldn't wait to be married. We decided to marry at the court-house, but still wanted to share our special day with family and friends. And I still wanted to wear the wedding dress I bought. So we planned a recep-tion for August 12 almost a year later, a date that would mark another significant event in our lives, when our son was born exactly two years later.

Supplies: alphabet (American Crafts); chipboard, patterned paper, trim, stickers (Crate Paper); doily (Martha Stewart Crafts); glitter glue (Ranger Industries); mini alphabet (Cosmo Cricket); paint (Ranger Industries); pearls (Recollections by Michaels); pen (Sakura Identi Pen); punches (Fiskars, EK Success); spray ink (Studio Calico); tile (Etsy Kenner Road)

## LEAF THANKS **CARD**

Cards not only make great personal gifts, but they also allow for creative play on a smaller scale. Plus, cards are a great way to practice or try out new techniques, such as hand-cut details, like these leaves. I inked the edges of the hand-cut details to make them stand out a bit more. This card can also carry many different sentiments on it thanks to the neutral leaves and colors.

Supplies: cardstock (Bazzill Basics Paper); ink (Ranger Industries); patterned paper (Fancy Pants Designs, Little Yellow Bicycle); punch (EK Success); stamp (Purple Onion Designs); twine (The Twinery)

Materials: floral patterned paper, scissors, paper piercer, pop-up adhesive, glitter glue

1 Cut out a detailed shape from the patterned paper using sharp scissors. Then cut out a coordinating motif from the patterned paper. Cut different elements out of the motif that you wish to highlight.

2 Roll the coordinating elements on the patterned paper piercer to give them a 3-D effect.

3 Place a pop-up adhesive on the back of the coordinating cutout and adhere it to the large motif.

4 Add accents to the cutout with glitter glue.

## more to love

Hand cut details look great when you choose to emphasize the pieces. Try adding stitches, glitter glue, ink or bling to make the details stand out. Add some distress by sanding the edges, or popping up certain sections. You can also cut away sections of the piece to reveal different shapes for a peek-a-boo effect.

# paper pleats

This technique evolved after I was watching a reality fashion TV show and was blown away by the beautiful ruffles and pleats in their outfits. With a punch, a piece of paper and a sewing machine (or glue!), you, too, can create these stunning pieces to accent your pages and papercrafts.

## STOR KLEM

The beauty of the Internet is that not only do we get to meet people from across the globe, we also get to learn about other cultures. I met Gudrun, a Norwegian scrapbooker, through a blog I ran. She taught me that in Norway, hugs are the norm, not kisses, and signed her notes with **Klemmer**, meaning hugs. And if there was deep affection, she would sign **Stor Klem**, meaning big hugs.

Supplies: alphabet (American Crafts, BasicGrey); digital frame (Stacked Frames); No 3 by Katie Pertiet (Designer Digitals); fabric strips (Studio Calico); ink (Ranger Industries); metal embellishment, paper flowers (The Girls' Paperie); patterned paper (3ndy Papir Co., Lily Bee Designs, Cosmo Cricket); pen (EK Success); punches (Martha Stewart Crafts); stamps (Purple Onion Designs); tags (Staples); walnut ink (Tsukineko); other: buttons

## CUPCAKES

These fun little treats are made from paper and trim. I stitched the paper pleats and then formed a cone shape gluing the edges together. I punched a circle and glued the cone shape to the punched circle. There are so many decorating ideas for these little cupcakes, including party decor. You also could build the base around a papier-mâché box and include a little birthday gift for someone special.

Supplies: patterned paper (Lily Bee Designs); trim (American Crafts, Maya Road); other: Styrofoam

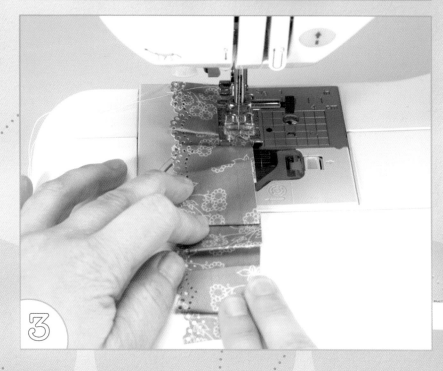

Materials: paper trimmer, patterned paper, lace punch, sewing machine and thread

1 Use a paper trimmer to cut a 1¾"×12" (4cm×30cm) strip of your favorite patterned paper. Punch along one side of the strip with a lace punch.

2 Starting at one edge, fold the strip back and forth on itself, creating a ruffled or pleated look. Make sure to fold the paper both ways, some folds to the left, and some to the right, to create an interesting texture.

3 Use a sewing machine to sew a straight stitch near the top of the strip to keep the folds in place.

## ruffle it up

You don't have to use a sewing machine to hold the shape of the ruffles. You can simply add some glue behind each pleat to create the same look. You can also use a variety of border punches to create different textures on the bottom of the ruffles. Want more drama? How about adding some bling or glitter glue to those pleats?

# embossed cardstock

Using punches and dies to emboss cardstock, or even patterned paper, is an innovative technique that is sure to please. It is completely addicting. You have been warned.

## THE BUTTERFLY EFFECT

People used to think Chrissi and I were twins despite us being born fifteen months apart. My mom said that we slept in the same crib because if I wasn't there, Chrissi would cry. We were hardly ever apart. I guess that is why I miss her so much; it feels like a part of me is missing. With a long title like, **The Butterfly Effect**, you tend to run out of letters quickly. So my solution with this layout was to use two complementary letter stickers.

Supplies: alphabet, rub-ons, spray ink, wood veneer (Studio Calico); alphabet (KI Memories); bobbin (Etsy Kenner Road); cardstock (Bazzill Basics Paper); patterned paper (Lily Bee Designs, Sassafras Lass, K&Company); patterned paper, stickers (October Afternoon); pen (Sakura Identi Pen); punches (EK Success, Martha Stewart Crafts); spray ink (Maya Road, Tattered Angels); stamps (Purple Onion Designs); stickers (Jenni Bowlin); thread (DMC); other: fabric

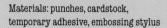

Materials: punches, cardstock, temporary adhesive, embossing stylus

1 Using a butterfly punch, cut out three butterflies from cardstock. Then cut out four 1¼" (4cm) circles using the circle punch.

2 Glue the butterflies and circles on the backside of the cardstock in a random pattern using temporary adhesive. Working on a hard surface, trace around each shape with a stylus, making a deep emboss. You will need to trace 2 or 3 times to get a defined emboss.

3 Flip over the cardstock and trace on the outside of the shapes making a deep reverse emboss. Again, you may need to trace the shape 2 or 3 times.

4 Remove the shapes from the back of the cardstock.

## more to emphasize

You can also use die-cuts or stickers to create the embossed cardstock look. Keep your punched shapes and die-cuts in a plastic bag ready to pull out at a moment's notice. You can cover the entire page with embossed shapes, or add in a design that really complements your story.

# edged borders

Got scraps? You can create these beautiful little moments around the edges of your layouts or projects just by adding little bits of patterned paper and embellishments. I tend to have scraps of paper laying around my desk that are begging to be used, and this technique is such an interesting way to frame your layout by using those scraps of patterned paper and embellishments.

## MAGICAL

I admit I am a complete geek about Harry Potter. I just love the magical world J.K. Rowling created. I have stood in line at midnight for the release of the books and movies. I also own a few Harry Potter shirts—Gryffindor, of course—all the movies and a journal. So when my husband, Andy, suggested adding a trip to the theme park, I was giddy with excitement. I am still thinking about the nonalcoholic butterbeer.

When I add journaling as a design element to my pages, I use a ruler and a pencil to draw a square frame onto the background and then journal around the edges, turning the paper as I write.

Supplies: alphabet (American Crafts); buttons, patterned paper (October Afternoon); paint (Ranger Industries); patterned paper (Cosmo Cricket, Lily Bee Designs); pen (Sakura Identi Pen); stickers (7 Gypsies); tab (BasicGrey); twine (The Twinery)

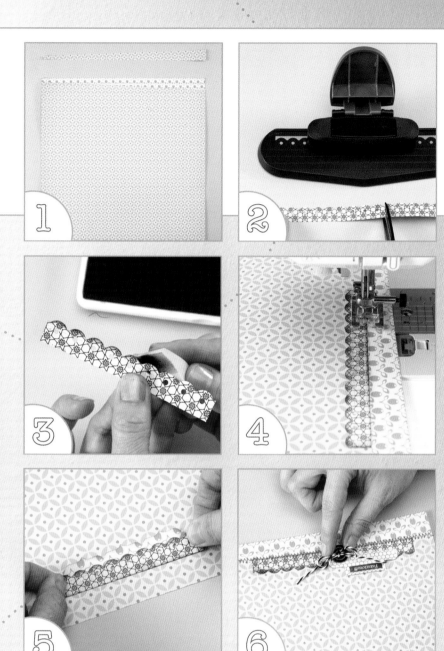

Materials: three pieces of coordinating patterned paper, paper trimmer, scissors, adhesive, border punches, black ink and sponge, sewing machine and thread, labels, button, twine

1 Place the background patterned paper in a paper trimmer at an angle and trim from the left corner with about 1" (4cm) cut off on the right. From the second patterned paper, cut a 1½"×12" (4cm×30cm) strip. Adhere that piece to the top of the background patterned paper, overlapping about ½" (13mm), making a 12"×12" (30cm×30cm) square.

2 Use a border punch to punch the third piece of coordinating patterned paper and trim into two pieces measuring 4" (10cm) and 5½" (14cm).

3 Brush the edges of the two strips with black ink using a sponge.

4 Adhere the 5½" (14cm) strip of patterned paper upside down on the upper right side of the background patterned paper, just below the second coordinating patterned paper. Using a sewing machine, stitch a zigzag stitch between the background patterned paper and the coordinating patterned papers at the top.

5 Take the 4" (10cm) strip of patterned paper and adhere it to the lower left corner of the background patterned paper.

6 Finish the border pieces with embellishments.

## over the top

This technique is a beautiful way to frame your layout, but you can also shift these groupings to the top of the layout so it peeks out of your albums. Really, you can add them to any side of your layout to add extra excitement.

# patterned paper peeks

I get so giddy when I find something unexpected or hidden in everyday treasures. It's like digging in a trunk in grandma's attic and finding all kinds of cool stuff. This simple technique is one of those hidden gems. By popping a pretty piece of contrasting patterned paper behind your layouts, you create beautiful layers that add a sense of wonder to your creations.

## LOVELY

When I was a kid, I use to think my grandma didn't like me. She seemed harder on me than the other grandkids. Later in life, I got to talk to her about it and she explained that she saw a lot of herself in me. What I believed to be dislike turned out to be a deep love. I am so happy that we shared that heart-to-heart before she passed away because I see her in such a different light now.

I started this layout with that lovely background paper and the blue labels cut out from patterned paper. I kept looking at the layout thinking it needed another pop of color. Blue and orange are complementary colors so adding in that touch of pinkish orange was just the pop I needed.

Supplies: brads (Making Memories); chipboard (Crate Paper); doily (Wilton Industries); embellishments (Pink Paislee); patterned paper (October Afternoon, Studio Calico, The Girls' Paperie); pen (Sakura Identi Pen); spray ink (Maya Road); stencil (The Crafter's Workshop)

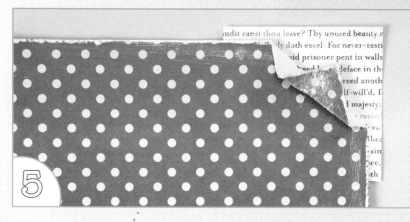

Materials: edge distresser, two patterned papers, craft knife, sand paper, glue stick

1 Use an edge distresser to distress the background patterned paper around the edges.

2 Cut a zigzag on the left edge of the pattern paper a ½" (13mm) in with a craft knife. Repeat this technique on the middle of the bottom edge. Cut two more jagged openings towards the center of the patterned paper.

3 Sand all edges of the background paper, including the cut openings, to give them a distressed look.

4 Bend the upper right corner of the background paper back towards the patterned paper. Then fold up a small piece from that corner and back again, creating a pleated corner. Adhere the pieces together using a glue stick.

5 Cut a few small pieces from the second patterned paper to place behind the tears and edges. Adhere them in place using a glue stick.

## piqued?

By using zigzag cuts, you can easily fold down the edges to get those peeks of patterned paper. You can make small cuts in your layouts or go bold by making some bigger cuts in the background. Try adding in a contrasting patterned paper behind the bold cut creating even more drama for your pages.

# tissue, fringed and cone paper flowers

Flowers are one of those embellishments that stand the test of time. I often try to mimic nature's creations with paper or transparencies. Here, you will see some of my favorite flower tutorials that will add the finishing touches to any of your pieces.

## SEWING TRINKET BOX

As I child, I always wanted to do things on my own. I was always wanting to learn. When I was six, I asked my momma to teach me to sew. I wanted more clothes for my baby doll. We couldn't always afford the ones from the store, so I decided to make them. She taught me to use the sewing machine and to create miniature outfits. I was always playing in her button jar looking for accessories. This little trinket box reminds me of all those little memories and how my love for sewing keeps growing.

Supplies: ATC Trinket Shadow Box, chandelier bead, chipboard, flowers, spray ink, stick pins, wood spools (Maya Road); brad, safety pins (Making Memories); brad (My Mind's Eye); chipboard, journal cards, patterned paper, stick pins, stickers, wood spools (Jenni Bowlin); chipboard, stickers (Crate Paper); drawer pull, metal corners (7 Gypsies); glass bottle, glass glitter, vintage bobbin (Etsy Kenner Road); paint, stamp ink (Ranger Industries); patterned paper (Lily Bee Designs); twine (The Twinery); other: vintage buttons, tissue paper, book paper

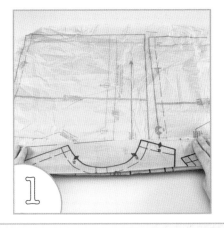

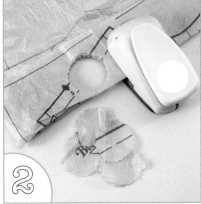

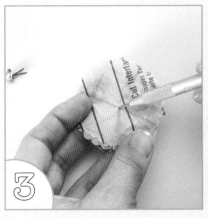

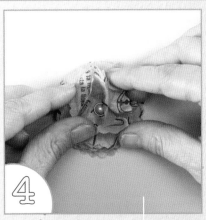

Materials: pattern tissue paper, scalloped punch, paper piercer, brad

## Tissue Flower

1 Using an old pattern tissue paper, fold tissue paper in half and then in half again. The fold width is determined by your punch size.

2 Using a scalloped circle punch, carefully slip the tissue paper into the punch and punch out four scalloped circles. Move the scalloped circle punch down the tissue paper and punch again to gather another four scalloped circles.

3 Stack all punched scalloped pieces of tissue paper together into one piece. Using a paper piercer, punch a small hole in the center of all eight scalloped circles and place the brad in the center of the scalloped circles.

4 Using your fingers, pull layer by layer, the scalloped tissue paper toward the center, scrunching the piece as you pull.

## paper love

This technique also works great using old book pages or dictionary pages. You can string lots of patterned papers and tissue papers on twine to make a fun home decor banner that can adorn any fireplace mantle, door frame, or window. Stream them along the ceiling for a new twist on party streamers.

continue to Fringed and Cone Paper Flowers >

Materials: patterned paper, circle punch, paper piercer, brad, scissors

## Fringed Flower

**1** Using a 2" (5cm) circle punch, cut out at least six circle punches of patterned paper.

**2** Stack all punched circle pieces of patterned paper together. Using a paper piercer, punch a small hole in the center of all six punched circles and place brad in the center of the circles. Attach the brad to the center.

**3** Using a pair of sharp scissors, cut from the outside of the circle towards the center of the circle creating a fringe around the entire circle.

**4** Using your fingers, pull the first layer of fringed punched circle toward the center. Keep repeating this technique, pulling up each layer towards the center.

## I HOPE YOU DANCE

I love adding flowers to layouts but on this one I didn't want them overwhelming the page. I first created the small paper flower using a textured patterned paper. The second flower toward the top was created using old book pages and the same technique I used on the tissue paper flower. Strips of patterned paper are another of my go-to designs in scrapbooking. For this layout I cut strips of patterned paper the same size, laid them next to each other and stitched them down.

Supplies: alphabet (BasicGrey); bling, cardstock, pen (American Crafts); chipboard, sheer die-cut (Maya Road); ink, paint (Ranger Industries); patterned paper (Basic Grey, Jenni Bowlin, Lily Bee Designs, Sassafras Lass); spray ink (Maya Road, Tattered Angels); stamp (Cocoa Daisy); trim (May Arts)

Materials: patterned paper, paper trimmer, pencil, Cone Flower template* (optional), scissors, liquid glue, paper piercer, brad

*Cone Flower template on page 122.

## Cone Flower

1 Using a paper trimmer, cut a 4"×4" (10cm×10cm) square from a piece of patterned paper. Using a pencil, draw a spiral shape circle from the outside edge to the center of the paper making a ½" (13mm) circle in the center (See Cone Flower template on page 122). Using sharp scissors, cut out the spiral starting at the outside edge and continuing toward the middle of the circle.

2 Working from the inside of the circle piece toward the outside, roll the paper piece around loosely creating a cone shape.

3 Apply liquid glue to the outside edge, pressing and holding the piece in place until the glue is dry.

4 Apply liquid glue to the center spiral piece and place the conical flower down on the center, holding it in place until the glue dries. Using a paper piercer, pierce a small hole in the center of the flower and attach the brad in the center.

# acetate flowers

After playing around with transparencies one day, I found that they can be molded. I wanted to make my flowers more three-dimensional so I thought if I heated the transparencies, I could make them bend. It's amazing what techniques you develop when you are willing to play around.

## GREAT LOVE **CANVAS**

I love starting out a canvas with bits of gesso, book paper and cheesecloth. Building up the background with bits of texture added interest into my mixed-media piece. I used a paintbrush with the spray ink to paint some of the background for the rich color and then sprayed it on the leftover chipboard pieces for another layer. (See **Soak It All In** on page 110.)

Supplies: canvas (Artist's Loft by Michaels); cardstock (American Crafts); filmstrip trim (Tim Holtz); font (Traveling Typewriter); gesso (Ranger Industries); spray inks (Maya Road); transparency (Hambly Screenprints); other: vintage buttons, tissue paper, book paper, cheese cloth

## LOVE NOTES **MINI ALBUM**

The flowers on the front of this mini album were created with a cool new product called "Clearly for Art." You can stamp or trace an image, then heat it up to make it flexible. I added a touch of alcohol ink to the clear flowers to make them stand out more. This mini album is ready to be filled with love notes from our family. With today's technologies, love notes come in so many forms, like Facebook wall posts, text messages, e-mails, instant messages, sticky notes and even old-fashioned love letters.

Supplies: alcohol ink, ink (Ranger Industries); alphabet, brads (BasicGrey); binder rings (Staples); patterned paper (Fancy Pants Designs, Jenni Bowlin, Collage Press, Glitz Designs, BasicGrey, Pink Paislee); postage stamps (Papier Valise); spray ink (Maya Road, Tattered Angels); transparencies (Hambly Screenprints, Wendy Vecchi Studio 490/Stampers Anonymous); watercolor paper (Strathmore)

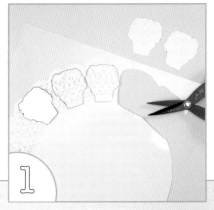

Materials: cardstock, pencil, scissors, black marker, white patterned transparency sheet, Petal Shape template* (optional), heat gun, clear liquid glue, black patterned transparency sheet, tweezers, button
*Petal Shape template on page 122.

1  Draw a flower petal similar to the shape of a lightbulb on a piece of cardstock and cut it out (See Petal Shape template on page 122). Trace four of the petal templates in black marker on the patterned transparency sheet. Cut out the petals by cutting just inside the traced black line with sharp scissors.

2  Use a heat gun to carefully heat the transparency petals, holding them with tweezers, until you are able to bend them.

3  Quickly bend the heated transparency petals into a waved shape, creating a bump toward the outer edge. Repeat this process for all four petals.

4  Cut out a small circle from the same colored transparency sheet for the base of the flower. Using clear liquid glue, adhere the bent transparency petals around the circle creating a poppy shape.

5  Cut out a small circle from the black transparency sheet and snip toward the center of the circle creating the center of the poppy. Carefully heat up the snipped black circle using tweezers until the transparency is bendable. Pull the snipped pieces toward center of the circle.

6  Lastly, adhere a button to the fringed circle.

## clearly more

For this technique, you can draw the petals on the backside of the transparency. Alcohol will rub off any excess black ink; put just a small amount on a cotton pad and gently rub the ink away. Be sure to use tweezers to hold your transparency shapes so you don't burn your fingers while using the heat gun. Make sure the tweezers have rubber grips, otherwise heat transfers up the metal.

# paper titles

Can't find the perfect color title for your layout? Try this technique for creating your own titles using patterned papers and a beloved font.

## CHANGING FAMILY

I love the contrasting horizontal and vertical lines on this layout. Even though there are more vertical lines, by using a horizontal photo and banner, I kept the focus on my family and the layout's story. My story is further told with the dangling embellishments found on the twine clothesline.

I wanted to emphasize my title, so I used a paper title with a bold font for the word changing. I decided to stitch the family title in a script font to show the how close we will always remain. This stitch technique can be found on page 56.

Supplies: alphabet stencil (Jillibean Soup); embellishments (7 gypsies, Tim Holtz, Maya Road, Canvas Corp., The Girls' Paperie); fabric strips (Studio Calico); glitter glue (Ranger Industries); patterned paper (Hambly Screenprints, My Mind's Eye, Jenni Bowlin, October Afternoon); punch (EK Success, Fiskars); spray ink (Maya Road); thread (DMC); twine (The Twinery)

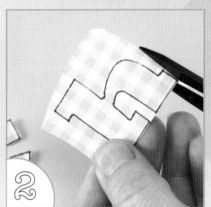

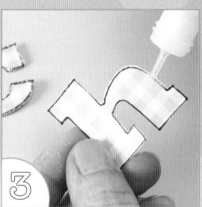

Materials: patterned paper, black pen, chipboard alphabet sheet, scissors, glitter glue

1 Trace your title onto patterned paper using a black pen and your favorite chipboard alphabet sheet as a stencil.

2 Cut out the letters from the patterned paper, cutting along the outside of the black lines. Make sure to keep the outlined edges for definition.

3 Apply a thin edge of glitter glue along the black traced edges.

## the written word

Want to add some excitement to your titles? Try stamping on your patterned paper first and then outlining your letters. Add flowers, buttons, or bling to those titles for more drama. Try mixing up the fonts and patterned papers to create a title that pops! Make sure you save those leftover chipboard alphabets (the negatives) to use as stencils for this technique and others you will find in the book.

2

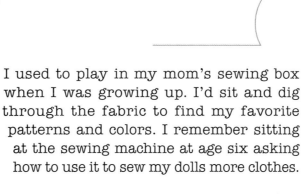

I used to play in my mom's sewing box when I was growing up. I'd sit and dig through the fabric to find my favorite patterns and colors. I remember sitting at the sewing machine at age six asking how to use it to sew my dolls more clothes.

My mom always said things like, "Slow and steady wins the race," or "The back of the project has to look as pretty as the front"—so I took my time with the stitches wanting to please her. Fast forward to years later and I added scrapbooking to my love of crafting. When I began crafting again, I was torn between which craft to dive into. Then I thought, "Why can't I use textiles on my page?" It made me sew happy (pun intended) to break out my needle and thread and start stitching on a page.

What I found was fabric added another layer to my pages. I dared to stitch through chipboard albums with reckless abandon. I embroidered and cross-stitched titles on my pages with fabric just like when I was a kid.

I hope you will see the beauty of adding fibers to your creations—adding titles out of felt, or fabric, using canvas pieces, making a grid pattern using either needle and thread, or a sewing machine, creating stitched designs, or hand-stitching a title on your page. Take my dare and try adding other crafts you love into your creations.

# fabric backgrounds

I could get lost in a fabric store, so many beautiful patterns and so many wonderful color combinations. The endless options make fabric the perfect accent for all your projects. In this technique we will be playing with sticky-backed canvases and mists to create movement and add excitement to your creations.

Supplies: canvas, gesso, ink, paint (Ranger Industries); patterned paper (Graphic 45); pen (American Crafts); stamp (Purple Onion Designs); wooden canvas (Artist's Loft by Michaels)

## CHEEKY BRITS

I met Nicky, Lisa and Laura through a scrap-booking message board. It's amazing how quickly I bonded with them, sharing the same dry sense of humor and love for scrapbook-ing. It was like we had been friends our entire lives, despite having never met. They always ask me, "Are you sure you aren't from the UK?"

Supplies: alphabet (American Crafts); alphabet, chipboard (Jenni Bowlin); die cuts (Cosmo Cricket); die cuts, spray mist, trim, trinket bead, trinket pins (Maya Road); flower (Prima Marketing); patterned paper (Cosmo Cricket); pen (Sakura Identi Pen); spray mist (Studio Calico, Tattered Angels), sticky-backed canvas (Ranger Industries); thread (DMC, JP Coats); trim (The Twinery, Maya Road); trinket bead, trinket pins (Maya Road); other: fabric

## FURNISHES A HOME
## WOODEN CANVAS

The same techniques I use on scrapbook layouts can extend to mixed-media arts and papercrafting. This wooden canvas was beg-ging to be painted and altered. I sketched out the chair on patterned paper and inked it up to give it the look of wood. Next, I used some sticky-backed canvas to create the cushions by stamping a damask image and then trimming it out to match the chair. The chair reminded me of my library, so I went searching for the perfect book quote.

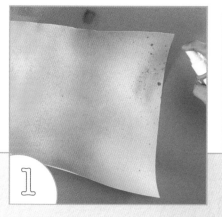

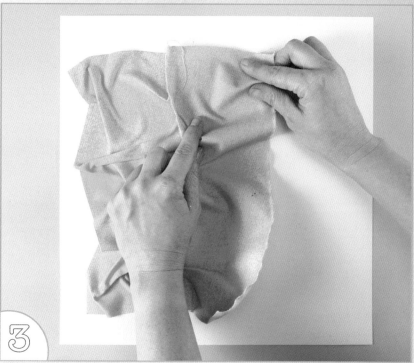

Materials: sticky-backed canvas, three spray inks or mists, scissors, white cardstock

1 Place a 12"×12" (30cm×30cm) piece of sticky-backed canvas in a box to avoid splatter when using the spray ink. Spray a 4" (10cm) vertical section on the left edge of the canvas with one color of the spray ink creating a misted look. Using a second color, spray another 4" (10cm) section down the center of the canvas. Spray the last 4" (10cm) section down the right side of the canvas with another color of spray ink.

2 Gently cut small snips into the 4" (10cm) sections with a pair of sharp scissors at the point where the color changes. Rip the 4" (10cm) canvas at these small snips, pulling in a downward motion, creating three separate pieces.

3 Scrunch the fabric into folds as you adhere the pieces onto the cardstock background, adjusting the folds as you go. Repeat this for all three pieces.

## sew much love

Once the canvas pieces are in place on the background, you can add in stitches between the 4" (10cm) pieces and around the edge. You can also add in some embroidery stitches for a really cool effect. Simple cross stitches in black would be dramatic, or you could stitch a little image that accents your story.

# fabric posies

Do you ever have bits of beautiful fabric left over that you just cannot part with? With this easy tutorial you can add your favorite fabric patterns to your page. Three layers of fabric, a needle and some thread can create this fabulous little posy to any of your creations.

## LONG AGO

This old photo is of my grandfather, his sister and his grandmother at his first communion. It brings so many questions to my mind about my grandfather's family. I don't know much about them, only that his grandmother was from Ireland. I would love to know more about their lives and their outfits—which I love—especially my grandfather's.

Supplies: alphabet (American Crafts); brads, patterned paper (My Mind's Eye); chipboard, kraft items, spray ink, trim, trinket pins (Maya Road); pearl bling (Prima Marketing); thread (DMC); other: fabric

Materials: three pieces of
coordinating fabric, scissors,
needle, floss, paper piercer, brad

1 Cut a 2" (5cm)
circle out of a
piece of fabric with
a pair of sharp
scissors. Then cut a
1¾" (4cm) circle out
of a second piece of
fabric, and a third
1½" (3cm) circle
from a third piece
of fabric. Stack all
three circles of fabric
on top of each other,
starting with largest
piece on bottom and
the smallest piece on
top.

2 With a needle
and floss, stitch
a running stitch
around the edge of
the smallest circle,
but stitching through
all three layers.

3 Gently pull the
floss, tightening
your stitches and
creating a ruffled
look to the flower.
Tie a knot in back to
secure the ruffles.

4 Pierce the center
of the fabric
flower using a paper
piercer and attach a
brad to complete the
posy.

## poised for more

Don't worry about making your circles
perfect. It's the imperfections that
make this flower so adorable. Pull the
thread tight for tighter ruffles or keep
it loose to see more of the fabric. Once
the circles are stitched together, twist
and turn the fabric to fluff your flower.

# felt titles

Let fashion inspire the fibers in your creations. While shopping for my teens, I noticed all the stitched titles on the graphic tees. I loved the look so much that I went home and created a layout using the same technique. You, too, can find inspiration in your everyday life.

## UP

My dad was the son of a racehorse jockey. Because of this job, my dad and his siblings spent most of their younger years traveling on the race track circuit. It's hard on a kid to travel so much and start over at each place. But no matter where they went, Chicago to Miami, they always had each other. I love this photo of the three of them standing in the front yard in Louisville, Kentucky, near Churchill Downs race track. It just amazes me to see my dad so young and to catch glimpses of his life through photos growing up.

Supplies: die cuts (Cosmo Cricket); felt flower, spray ink (Maya Road); ink, paint (Ranger Industries); patterned paper (3ndy Papir Co, Crate Paper); patterned paper, spray ink (Studio Calico); pen (EK Success); spray ink (Tattered Angels); thread (DMC); tin (Jenni Bowlin); trim (Strano Designs)

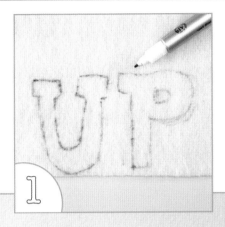 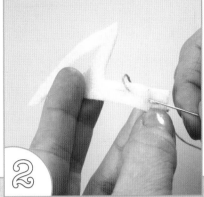

Materials: cream felt, black pen, scissors, needle, floss, liquid glue

1 Lightly draw a title onto felt with a black pen.

2 Using sharp scissors, cut along the inside of the black lines to cut out the letters. Thread four strands of floss through the needle. Carefully backstitch down the center of each felt letter, taking care not to pull or stretch the felt out of shape. Using liquid glue, adhere the title to the page.

## it felt so good

When I stitch on my pages, my momma is always in my head saying, "the back needs to look as pretty as the front." So I tend to use a backstitch on my creations. It keeps the stitches straight and my backs do look as pretty as the fronts.

These beautiful titles look great in fabric, too. Adhere some of your favorite fabric to white cardstock using a glue stick, then trace your title on the fabric. You can stitch or use glitter glue to accent the edges.

Take a closer look at the metal flower on the layout. I snipped a tart tin and hammered down the edges. Next, I added a white flower (seen above) and used spray inks and a paintbrush to color the thread and pearl.

# ruched flower

What is more beautiful than gorgeous fabric patterns? Well, seeing them come to life in pleats and ruffles in this ruched flower of course. All you need is a needle, thread and fabric to create these fabulous little flowers that can accent any project.

## DAYS GONE BY

I love, love this photo of my mom, my sister Chrissi and me. It makes me laugh because it captures our personalities so well. Chrissi was the goofy one. Sometimes she would change one of her socks when our mom's back was turned and then announce that, "Chrissi no here, I am Pinky Tuscadero." I, on the other hand, was always the shy one. But from that little smirk on my face, you can see there was always something churning in my head.

The background of this project is created the same way as in the **Chipboard Collage** on page 66. You can also make ruched flowers using patterned paper. After stitching the strip of patterned paper, spray the paper with a tiny bit of water and gently pull the thread, keeping in mind you have to be very careful not to tear the paper.

Supplies: alphabet, patterned paper, wood frame (Studio Calico); buttons, stickers (October Afternoon); chipboard letters (The Girls' Paperie); die cut, spray ink (Maya Road); gesso (Ranger Industries); pen (Sakura Identi Pen); stencil (The Crafter's Workshop); stickers (Crate Paper); tag (Staples); thread (DMC); other: fabric

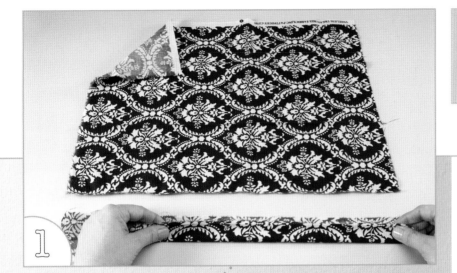

Materials: fabric, scissors, floss, needle, cardstock, circle punch, liquid glue, button

1. Use sharp scissors to make a small snip 2" (5cm) from the edge of a 17" (43cm) piece of fabric. Rip off the strip of fabric where you snipped, pulling in a downward motion to create a frayed edge. Fold the 2"×17" (5cm×43cm) strip of frayed fabric in half widthwise.

2. Stitch a running stitch in a zigzag pattern down the length of the frayed fabric piece using a needle and floss.

3. Once you reach the end of the frayed fabric, gently pull the floss to tighten your stitches and create the ruched look. Keep the needle threaded for Step 5.

## stitched with love

You can choose a neutral color of thread for a nice little accent, or go bold and pick a complementary color to really stand out. Create a ruched flower with a twist—try stitching together some scraps of fabrics and then use the same technique.

4. Punch a small circle out of cardstock and use liquid glue to adhere the ruched flower to the center of the circle, turning the fabric into a circle.

5. Place a button on top and stitch it to the ruched flower.

# meandering twine

One day I was playing around with ribbon when it wandered around my page so organically that I knew right then I had to stitch it down for fear of losing that creative goodness. Now that process has become a staple in my ribbon techniques. I love seeing ribbon curl around in circles on a page, weaving through photos, texts and layers of paper.

Supplies: alphabet (American Crafts); floss (DMC); flower die cuts, stickers, patterned paper (Sassafras Lass); paint (Ranger Industries); paper fastener (7 Gypsies); pen (Sakura Identi Pen); spray mist (Tattered Angels); twine (Cocoa Daisy); other: buttons, fabric tissue paper

## OFF-CENTERED

I think it's funny how almost all the family photos we have from our younger years are completely off-center. My mom says that is how she knows my Grandma Tucci had the camera—she never could take the picture straight on. But while she may not have been the best photographer, she made up for the off-kilter pictures by being our favorite cook.

There are lots of ways to add texture to a layout. By simply adding tissue paper to the background using gel medium or layering border stickers, you can add another dimension to your layout. Bring in items that have meaning. The tissue paper, for example, reminds me how my mom would make all of our clothes when we were younger.

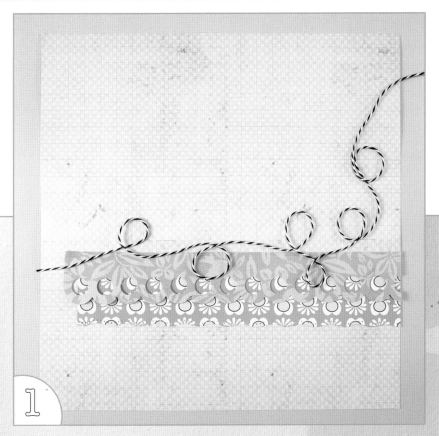

Materials: thin ribbon or twine, paper piercer, needle

1 Gently layer the twine across the page letting it fall in an organic manner creating loops and swirls.

2 Using a paper piercer, create small stitching holes along the loops and length of the twine.

3 Thread your needle with the same twine and tack the twine down using the pierced holes to hold it in place.

## like to wander

Keep in mind the type of twine or ribbon when you are working on your layouts. While twine loves to loop, some thicker ribbons have folds and bumps. In other words, let the ribbon or twine determine the look on your page. You can easily tack the ribbon or twine with bits of liquid glue or add in some contrasting cross-hatched stitching to give it a unique look. Check out **Mustache Love** on page 108.

# ruffled ribbon

Like most scrapbookers, I am a ribbon junkie. I love all the colors, the patterns and the variety of trims. You can enhance any of your projects with these beautiful ruffled ribbon flowers. With a simple needle, thread and your favorite ribbon, you can make these lovely flowers to accent any of your projects.

## SWEET THINGS

I love making home decor for my home. This little frame is intended to brighten up our guest bedroom. Flowers may fade, but these little blooms will always radiate beauty. You don't have to choose colors to complement the room but instead pick colors you will always love.

The background was created using layers of gesso. I applied both paint and spray ink to the gesso background, like the **Splatters of Paint** technique found on page 120. The little circles were simply created using the lid of the spray ink container pressed into the background.

Supplies: bingo card, vintage seam binding (Etsy Kenner Road); buttons (Jenni Bowlin, Tim Holtz); canvas (Artist's Loft by Michaels); gesso, paint (Ranger Industries); lace trim, patterned paper (The Girls' Paperie); paint (Liquitex); pen (Sakura Identi Pen); spray ink (Maya Road); stencil (The Crafter's Workshop); trim (Strano Designs); other: frame

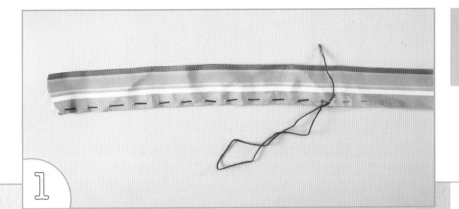

1 Thread a needle with a long piece of floss and knot one end. Stitch a running stitch along the bottom edge of a piece of ribbon that is approximately 18" (46cm) long.

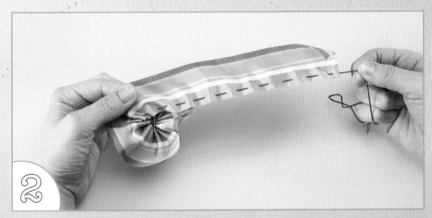

2 Gently pull the floss, tightening your stitches and giving the ribbon a ruffled look.

3 Punch a small circle out of cardstock and use liquid glue to adhere the ruffled ribbon flower to the center of the circle.

4 Sew a coordinating button to the center of the ruffled ribbon flower.

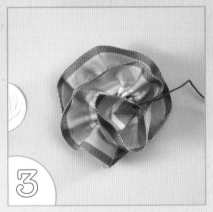

## ruffled up?

This technique works for all kinds of fibers, especially thin or thick ribbon or fabric. Try using some lace or crochet trim for a cool vintage-looking flower. After creating your long running stitch, try snipping the top of the ribbon every ¼" (6mm) being careful not to cut your thread. This creates a beautiful fringed ruffled ribbon flower.

# stitched through ribbon

Have you ever really looked at your favorite items and deconstructed what you truly love about them? For me it seems to be those unexpected touches that add just a little bit of flavor to the piece. By stitching through ribbons on your projects, you can add that bit of surprising detail, that zing that really finishes off your creations.

## TREAT

There are so many subtle details in this layout that invite you to take a closer look. The bottom layers were created with patterned paper and stickers layered on top of each other. I had leftover green strips of paper that I used to punch the circles that are scattered across the background and at the top of the layout. The circles on the green background paper are popped up with 3-D adhesive.

Supplies: bingo card, chipboard (Jenni Bowlin); buttons (October Afternoon); cardstock (American Crafts); flowers, metal embellishment, stickers, trim, patterned paper (The Girls' Paperie); paint (Ranger Industries); pen (Sakura Identi Pen); punch (EK Success); thread (DMC); twine (The Twinery)

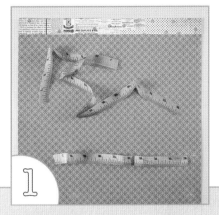

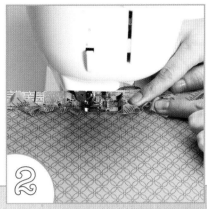

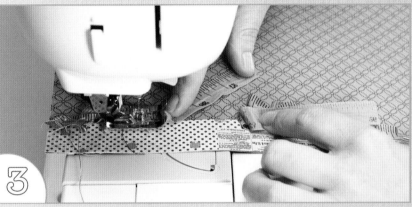

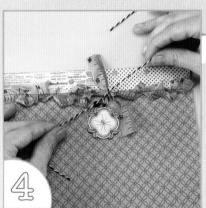

Materials: ribbon, scissors, patterned paper, sewing machine and thread, charm, twine

1 Take a 36" (91cm) piece of ribbon and cut it into 2 pieces, one 26" (66cm) long and the other 10" (25cm) long.

2 Starting at left edge of the patterned paper, machine-stitch the longer piece (26"[66cm]) of ribbon across the paper to the right using a straight stitch and scrunching up the ribbon as you go. Leave a 2" (5cm) piece of the ribbon unstitched.

3 With the shorter piece of ribbon (10"[25cm]), start at the right edge of the patterned paper and stitch to the left until you meet the other ribbon, again leaving a 2" (5cm) piece of ribbon unstitched.

4 Tie the 2" (5cm) of ribbon from both pieces in a single knot. Then tie the charm to the twine and tie that to the stitched ribbon knot. Tie the stitched ribbon one more time, securing the charm in place.

## hungry for more?

You can add a little or a lot of ribbon to the page. Thin ribbon makes a great border, while thick ribbon adds a dramatic accent. Try tying a bow with your ribbon before stitching it down. Be sneaky and use two pieces of stitched ribbon leaving room to place a photo in the space. That gives the appearance that the ribbon is under the picture without the bulk of the ribbon. Does the background look familiar on this piece? Check out **Edged Borders** on page 20.

# paper appliqué

My momma makes the most beautiful quilts. I am always wowed by appliqué pieces. This technique is my version of a reverse appliqué. First you will create beautiful stitches, either by machine or by hand, and then you will add in your favorite patterned paper to give those stitches some pop.

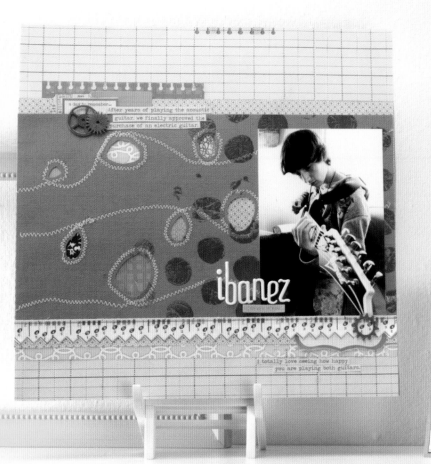

Supplies: alphabet (American Craft); cardstock (Bazzill Basics Paper); tulle flower (Prima Marketing); patterned paper (BasicGrey, October Afternoon, My Mind's Eye, Lily Bee Designs, Pink Paislee); stencil (The Crafter's Workshop); sticker (Crate Paper)

## IBANEZ

Anthony very rarely lets me photograph him. Because of this, it has been a struggle to document his growth these past few years. But now that he has his guitar, he is much happier to be photographed. He often walks around the house with both of his guitars, strumming new tunes and old songs he loves. He fills our house with music, and I am overjoyed that he has found his passion.

Supplies: alphabet (American Crafts); cardstock (Bazzill Basics Paper); embellishments (Tim Holtz); font (Traveling Typewriter); patterned paper, stickers (Lily Bee Designs, Studio Calico, Crate Paper); patterned paper (Sassafras Lass); punch (EK Success); spray ink (Maya Road); other: bubble wrap

## FRIEND **CARD**

This sweet little card is another way to create stitched cutouts. First, I traced the flower from a stencil onto the kraft cardstock. Next, I stitched the petals of the flower and cut out the insides using a craft knife. After placing the patterned paper behind the petals, I decided to cut out the flower and adhere it to a neutral background. To complete the flower, I added a premade tulle flower to the center.

Materials: paper trimmer, cardstock, sewing machine and thread, patterned paper, craft knife, cutting mat, glue

1 Using a paper trimmer, cut a piece of cardstock to 6"×12" (15cm×30cm). Using a sewing machine, stitch a zigzag stitch across the length of the page creating loops in the lines of stitching. Repeat this process until you have created three lines. Try to make the loops appear randomly placed.

2 Carefully cut out the cardstock from the centers of the stitched loops using a cutting mat and craft knife.

3 Cut small pieces of patterned paper and adhere them to the backside of the centers loop so that the pattern shows through.

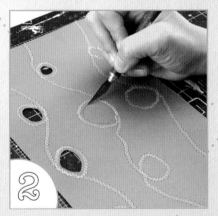

## sew much to love

Momma always says, "Slow and steady wins the race," so when you are pressing that petal down, go nice and slow to get those beautiful stitches. The cool thing about this technique is you can add anything behind those stitches, ribbon, fabric, patterned paper, or even fill them in with bits of glitter.

# playful banners

Banners are a huge trend that I don't see going away, at least not for a while. This technique allows you the freedom to create these stellar pieces from supplies you already have close at hand.

## GRADUATION CAKE

My sweet daughter graduated from high school in 2011. I thought I could turn a Styrofoam cake into an adorable centerpiece for the party since I was serving cupcakes instead of a cake. I decided to hang a banner between two wooden skewers using her school colors as inspiration. The banner is a perfect touch to any cake, real or Styrofoam, for many parties and functions.

Supplies: flowers (Petaloo); patterned paper (3ndy Papir Co, Lily Bee Designs); punch (EK Success); stickers (Jenni Bowlin); tissue embellishment (Martha Stewart Crafts); trim (May Arts, Maya Road, My Mind's Eye); twine (The Twinery); other: Styrofoam

## THIS GIRL

There is a story told quite often in my family of how my younger sister, Chrissi, when she was a toddler, bit a dog on the nose after he growled at her. Supposedly, there is proof of the incident in a picture somewhere. I found the photo while I was browsing through some of the family slides only to realize it wasn't Chrissi who bit the dog—it was me!

This banner is so easy to create using your leftover supplies. A little baby powder on the back of your stickers removes the adhesive so they can just dangle from the twine. These banners are not only great on a scrapbook layout but make really cute home or birthday party decor.

Supplies: alphabet stickers, die cuts (Cosmo Cricket); buttons, chipboard, patterned paper, stickers (Crate Paper); pen (Sakura Identi Pen); trim (Maya Road); twine (The Twinery)

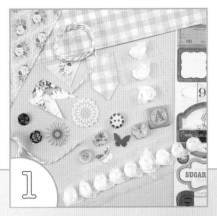

Materials: cardstock shapes, rose ribbon, patterned paper, scissors, baby powder, labels, twine, buttons, needle, paper piercer

1 Collect pieces, like stickers, scraps of patterned paper, cardstock shapes, etc., to use on the banner. You can also snip individual rosettes from ribbons to use in the banner. Three of each set of embellishments is always a good number to start with.

2 Sprinkle baby powder on the backsides of label stickers to remove the adhesives.

3 Cut a long length of twine for the base of the banner. Tie one end of twine in a bow in the center of a button.

4 Using a paper piercer, punch two holes in each of the objects. Thread a needle onto the twine and stitch through the pieces to create the banner.

5 Thread one end of the banner through the last button and tie a bow in the center of the button. Trim the ends of the twine using scissors.

## string me along

Punch out some shapes to repeat on a banner like butterflies or hearts. Go digging in your button tin and use a variety of shapes and colors along a piece of twine. Or simply cut out different pennant pieces from patterned paper. Give your banners some lift by using some pop up adhesive. Create a beautiful banner using bling and a pen to "string" them together.

# stitched journaling

A great way to accent your story is by simply adding a few stitches to your journaling. Why stop there? In this technique you will find ways to really emphasize your tale by adding in some embossed lines and beautiful colored stitches.

## ONE STEP

To me, the story is just as important as the design, so if I can highlight it in special ways, I will. On this particular layout, I love how embossing and stitching the journal lines really accents my journaling. I discovered after poking the holes for stitching that I poked one too many. This happy little accident allowed me to add in the french knots of color.

Supplies: alphabet sticker (Lily Bee Designs); button, patterned paper (Cosmo Cricket); cardstock (Bazzill Basics Paper); chipboard (Maya Road); crackle medium (Helmar USA); flowers (Papier Valise); gesso, spray ink (Ranger Industries); pen (EK Success); punches (Martha Stewart Crafts, Fiskars); spray ink (Maya Road, Tattered Angels); thread (DMC); washi tape (Hambly Screenprints); other: fabric

1

2

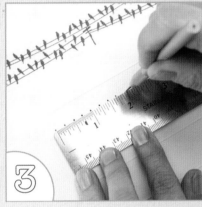

3

4

had some major ups and downs these past few years

things needed to change in my life but change is

ry, especially when you look at the big picture.

Materials: cutting mat, cardstock, pencil, ruler, scoring board, bone folder, paper piercer, black pen, needle, floss

1 Mark nine lines on the backside of the cardstock approximately 6" (15cm) across the page and 1" (3cm) apart using a pencil and ruler.

2 Score these penciled lines on the backside of the cardstock using a scoring tool or bone folder to create an embossed line.

3 Flip the cardstock over and use a ruler and paper piercer to pierce holes in between the embossed lines ¼" (6mm) apart.

4 Using a black pen, journal your story right above the pierced holes, or embossed lines—your choice.

5 With floss and needle, stitch a running stitch in the pierced holes.

## knot it

Play around with your stitches. Try using a continuous stitch with no spaces between, cross-stitches, or even a chain stitch. Another cool idea is to use two or three different threads in one stitch. With floss, it is easy to pull apart the individual threads and combine them to create a spectacular look. Miscounted your pierced holes? No problem—throw in some french knots in coordinating colors to fill in those extra bits.

# stitched grid

The grid is my go-to design. I love the possibilities it presents, whether you use one big photo with a grid in the background or multiple photos filling in the grid spaces. You can always hand-stitch or machine-stitch your grid to get different looks.

Supplies: alphabet (American Crafts); chipboard (Maya Road); die cuts (Cosmo Cricket); paint (Ranger Industries); patterned paper (Cosmo Cricket, October Afternoon); pen (Sakura Identi Pen); thread (DMC)

## OH, THE PLACES WE GO!

I didn't start traveling until I was twenty-seven years old. I am still amazed by all the places I have been, thanks to my very generous in-laws and having a pilot for a husband. We have made a point to make traveling a priority in our lives. And with each new place we visit, we bring something home with us—something new we learned about the world's different cultures.

## JOY **MINI ALBUM**

This holiday mini album was cre-ated using gesso and spray ink on the front cover. I then stitched a grid pattern using my sewing machine. I used a medium-sized needle to stitch through the chipboard making sure I went slowly so I didn't jam the thread.

Supplies: alphabet (American Crafts); chipboard album, spray inks (Maya Road); embellishments (Making Memories); gesso (Liquitex); patterned paper, flower, sticker (The Girls' Paperie)

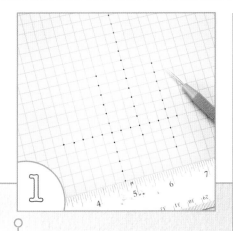

Materials: ruler, paper piercer, needle, floss, grid patterned paper, chipboard pieces

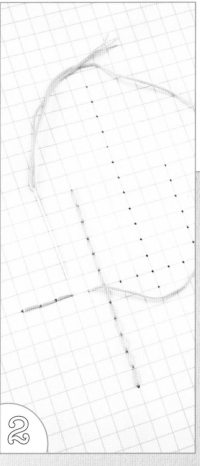

1 Use a paper piercer to pierce holes ¼" (6mm) apart in vertical lines down the page, starting and stopping at various points. Then pierce holes ¼" (6mm) apart in horizontal lines across the page, starting and stopping at various points. Use a ruler to measure and align the holes.

2 Stitch a series of backstitches across these lines with a needle and floss, creating a grid pattern.

3 Embellish the squares using patterned paper, buttons and chipboard pieces.

## keep going!

Sometimes I will create a grid in the background and then purposely place my pictures and embellishments over the grid. Keep in mind that you can vary the distance between your lines to create bigger or smaller squares. Another interesting way to play with the grid is to place the grid at the top and bottom of your page and then place your photos in the center of the page away from the grids.

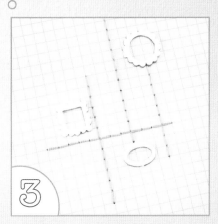

# stitched titles

When I think about this technique, it reminds me of sitting as a kid with the family, embroidering a pillow case or dish towel. Now I sit with my own kids, still stitching away.

## GROUNDED

Every year I create a birthday layout. I didn't start these types of pages until I was 36 and now I wish I had done it when I was younger, too. Sometimes the layout is just a simple list documenting events of the past year. Other times it is deep journaling about who I am, where I am going and everything in between. I want the next generation to know who I am and I figure, since I know me best, the birthday layouts I create can do just that.

Supplies: buttons (Cosmo Cricket, Making Memories); buttons, chipboard, pins, rub-on (Jenni Bowlin); chipboard (American Crafts, The Girls' Paperie); gesso (Ranger Industries); mist, pins (Maya Road); patterned paper (October Afternoon); punches (Martha Stewart Crafts); tags (Etsy The Living Room Floor, Staples); thread (DMC); washi tape (Hambly Screenprints); wire (Stampin' Up!)

## SEW WHAT **CARD**

I am a punny and dorky girl. This card is a perfect example of my twisted sense of humor and totally makes me laugh. I love how the embellishments accent the phrase. To create the ticket card, simply use a circle punch and punch a quarter of the paper off the corners.

Supplies: alphabet (Cosmo Cricket); fabric (Amy Butler); patterned paper (Hambly Studios, My Mind's Eye, Lily Bee Designs, October Afternoon); pins, wood embellishments (Maya Road); punch (EK Success)

1

2

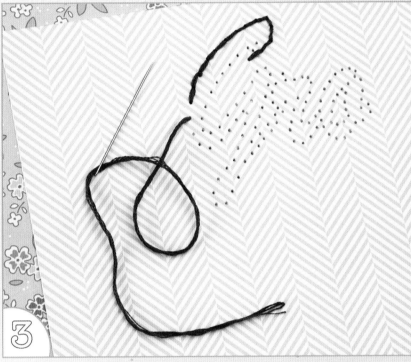

3

Materials: printed title on transparency sheet (acetate), patterned paper, paper piercer, craft mat, needle, floss

1 Print out the title you want to use on your page on a piece of transparency.

2 Place the printed title on patterned paper. Using a paper piercer and craft mat, pierce the title, making small holes around the outline of the words.

3 Stitch a series of backstitches through the pierced holes starting at the beginning of the title. Stitch it as you would write it, otherwise you may get confused on which stitch goes where. Be careful not to pull too hard on the stitches so you don't tear the patterned paper.

## sew easy!

Punch and stitch the titles like you would write the word so you know how the holes line up. If the open font gets too confusing, try using a simple font first and then move on to the complicated fonts. Practice makes perfect, so why not try these looks out on tags that can be added later to any project? Remember to keep all those printed titles by hole-punching one side and placing them on a binder ring, ready to use at a moment's notice. If you find a font you like, why not print out multiple generic titles on a single page to use so you save your paper or transparency in that font. Make sure when you are printing on transparencies you have the sheets made especially for your printer, which can be found at your local office supply store.

art of embellishments

I am a self-admitted embellishment junkie. I have jars, drawers and tins full of fun little embellishments. I have a plethora of stickers and rub-ons in canvas totes. I have clear jars full of buttons in their rainbow coordinated order. There are flowers and brads blooming all over my shelves. I have oodles and oodles of chipboard and acrylic accents. And I definitely don't need to start talking about my drawers full of alphabets. So, one can say I am a hoarder, an obsessed embellishment hobbyist. I don't throw anything away for that one day when it may be the perfect embellishment for my page. I like to think of it as planning ahead because you never know when you may need that sparkly sequin on your project.

Embellishments are just like shoes—I don't think a girl can have too many label stickers in every color. I keep two vintage dessert cups on my table filled with little bits and baubles that are always up for rotation. With these embellishments at my fingertips, I find it easier to tuck them here and there on my pages. If I see them, then I will use them.

In this chapter, I want you to start giving embellishments a new life. I want you to think of them more as an extension of your story than just a pretty little piece that helps make a lovely page. We'll start with some simple rub-on techniques including layering, bordering and popping them up to give a new dimension. I'll show you how to use leftover chipboard pieces to create stunning backdrops, how to tuck in embellishments to patterned paper layers and fabric. It will become second nature to you as you add those bits to your journaling to truly accent the story you're out to tell. Embellishing your titles deserve some attention, too, so we'll take a look at how to give them a bit more zing.

# layered rub-ons

A simple rub-on is a beautiful addition to any project, so why not add two or three? This technique is a great way to use up leftover supplies while adding beautiful elements to a page. By layering rub-ons, you can create stellar backdrops for your stories and artwork.

## ATC CARDS

ATCs, or Artist Trading Cards were originally invented to mail to other artists. I find them to be perfect little canvases to practice new techniques, as they don't feel as overwhelming as larger pieces. Traditionally the size of baseball cards, these ATCs are slightly larger so I can show the layers a bit more clearly.

Supplies: brad (Making Memories); cardstock (American Crafts); embellishment, rub-ons (7 Gypsies); glitter glue (Ranger Industries); pin, spray ink (Maya Road); rub-ons, spray ink (Studio Calico); rub-ons (Hambly Screenprints); rub-ons, stencil (Jenni Bowlin); stencil (The Crafter's Workshop); stickers (Cosmo Cricket); twine (The Twinery); other: buttons

## SEASON DELIGHTS

I love using bits of nontraditional colors for my seasonal layouts. In this particular layout, it's the blue found in the rub-ons. I started this layout with a floral green patterned paper and toned it down with some gesso. After spritzing the page with some mists, I began building up my layers with rub-ons. Those trees stacked over one another added the perfect accent to my seasonal layout.

Supplies: alphabet (BasicGrey); buttons (Jenni Bowlin); flower (The Girls' Paperie); gesso (Liquitex); patterned paper (Fancy Pants Designs, The Girls' Paperie); pen (American Crafts); rub-ons (Fancy Pants Designs); spray ink (Maya Road)

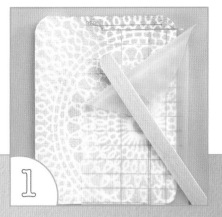

1

2

3

4

Materials: cardstock, multiple rub-ons, rub-on tool, labels, glitter glue, brad, paper piercer

1 Starting with a misted cardstock ATC, rub on a grid background to the right side of the card.

2 Layer the neutral-colored star rub-ons toward the center of the card, overlapping the grid, and rub into place. Next, cut out a red flower rub-on and place it on top of the gray grid rub-on and rub the red flower on.

3 In the upper left corner, rub on a pink cloud close to the top. Next, layer on a gray cloud to the upper left corner, overlapping the pink cloud with the left edge.

4 Add your additional rub-ons and embellishments. Highlight your favorite rub-ons with glitter glue.

## rub it on!

When layering rub-ons, you don't have to have matching rub-ons. The more contrasting the rub-ons are, the better, because each layer takes on a life of its own. Trim the rub-ons from their packaging and hover over an area to find the perfect placement.

# edged rub-ons

Rub-on borders add a lot of interest to the page when they are added slyly. Tie them together by layering the rub-ons and stitching a frame around the patterned paper.

## THE EVERYDAY ART OF MYKONOS

The Greek Island of Mykonos was such a fabulous location for a photo junkie like me. There was so much eye candy all over the place, that I was hardly ever seen without a camera in my face. Everywhere I turned, I was blown away by the sheer beauty of the island.

Originally, I had planned to place the pictures in more of a grid pattern. After adhering all the rub-ons around the page, I began carelessly tossing the photos onto the page. I looked down to notice how beautifully arranged they ended up and decided to keep them that way with a few minor adjustments. I love happy little accidents.

Supplies: alphabets (Jillibean Soup, Cosmo Cricket); patterned paper (Crate Paper); rub-ons (Studio Calico, Hambly Screenprints, Jenni Bowlin)

Materials: patterned paper, multiple rub-ons, rub-on tool, sewing machine and thread

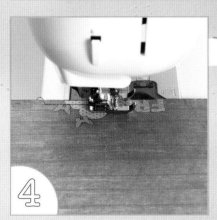

1  Rub on the first red colored rub-on at the edge of the patterned paper at the top and bottom left corners. Rub on a gray rub-on at the upper right corner and down the left side.

2  Layer green and pink rub-ons at the upper right corner, slightly overlapping the gray rub-on. Layer a yellow rub-on and a black rub-on on top of the grey rub-on at the left side of the page.

3  Add the green day-of-the-week rub-on at the bottom center. Layer pink and yellow rub-ons at the bottom center, slightly overlapping each other.

4  Randomly machine-stitch using a black straight stitch through some of the rub-ons.

## around the edge

Try to use contrasting colored rub-ons so they stand out a bit more. Find rub-ons in your supplies that support your stories. On my layout, the month relates to my travel date and the Polaroid image to all the photos I was taking.

# 3-D rub-ons

Give rub-ons a new life by adding them to painted chipboard or popping them up on your pages.

## 3 PUPS

I never thought I would own one Chihuahua, let alone three. These pups are very dear to my heart and provide our whole family such joy. I wanted to capture the whimsy and personality of each of them, hence the outdoorsy feel to this layout. You will see lots of hand-cut details on this layout. The kitelike tailings took some time to hand cut, but, to me, it was worth it. The yellow flowers scattered across the page are another hand-cut detail. See **Not So Typical** on page 14.

Supplies: alphabet (Pink Paislee); bling (Me & My Big Ideas); buttons, patterned paper (Cosmo Cricket); flower, patterned paper, rub-on, spray ink (Studio Calico); metal number (Tim Holtz); patterned paper (October Afternoon, Jenni Bowlin); rub-on (Hambly Screenprints)

## MR. AND MRS. **CARD**

When I saw this camera rub-on, I thought it would make a really cute wedding card. I placed the rub-on on vanilla cardstock, cut it out, and adhered pop-up adhesive to the back. I wanted just a tiny bit of color, so I layered multiple trim pieces with the tiny bit of teal patterned paper peeking from behind the trim.

Supplies: cardstock (Bazzill Basics Paper); patterned paper (Cosmo Cricket, Fancy Pants Designs); rub-on (Hambly Screenprints); sticker (Crate Paper); trim (Maya Road)

Materials: chipboard, foam brush, white paint, rub-ons, rub-on tool, scissors, pop-up adhesive

1 Using a foam brush, paint a piece of chipboard white.

2 Rub on the butterflies and clouds to the white painted chipboard.

3 Using sharp scissors, cut out the rub-on shapes from the chipboard.

4 Place them randomly on the page, adding pop-up adhesive on some of the pieces to give them even more dimension.

## keep going

Take those 3-D rub-ons a bit further by adding some bling, glitter or metal accents to the pieces. Try painting a bright color on the chipboard for a completely different look. You can even carefully add in some stitches to those rub-ons before adding the pop-up adhesive.

# chipboard collage

Are you a collector of chipboard alphabets like me? You can make those favorite fonts go further by using up those loveable leftovers in a chipboard collage. This versatile technique is great for any creative project—canvases, mini albums or even your scrapbook layouts.

## YOUR HEART **CANVAS**

One day, I was playing around with paint and clear embossing powder. When I was using the heat gun, paint started to bubble up and almost crackle with the embossing powder. My first reaction was panic, but that soon turned to deep satisfaction at this cool new look. Now it is one of my favorite paint techniques. After placing the banner quote across the heart, I decided it was still a bit too plain to stand up next to the heart. I decided to add a darker glitter glue to the edge. It was the perfect finishing touch.

Supplies: cardstock (American Crafts); chipboard (The Girls' Paperie); clear embossing powder, glitter glue, paints (Ranger Industries); font (Freestyle Script); gesso, matte medium (Liquitex); sequins (Doodlebug Design)

## GOOD THINGS **MINI ALBUM**

It is easy to take for granted all the blessings in my life, but I always want to be thankful. This simple mini album holds 4"×6" (10cm×15cm) photos of all I am grateful for in my life, like friends, family and art.

Supplies: alphabet (American Crafts, Studio Calico); binder rings (Staples); paint (Ranger Industries); patterned paper (Echo Park Paper, Lily Bee Designs, BasicGrey, Collage Press); spray ink (Maya Road); stickers (Studio Calico); trim (Strano Designs)

Materials: gesso, palette knife, canvas, chipboard letters, paint palette, paints, paintbrush, water, cloth, Clear UTEE, heat gun

1 Using a palette knife, spread a layer of gesso over the entire canvas.

2 Working quickly, add random chipboard letters into the gesso pressing slightly to make sure the letters sink in a bit. Add more gesso to areas that need a bit of extra texture. Let the piece dry.

3 Using a paintbrush and watered-down acrylics, add color to the canvas, wiping off the excess paint from the letters.

4 Pat the excess paint off for distressed areas between the letters.

5 Sprinkle Clear UTEE onto small areas of wet paint. Using a heating gun, heat set the Clear UTEE until the paint begins to bubble, adding even more texture. Add in more acrylic paint colors and repeat the process for a unique look.

## mix it up

Try using the same font, or mix up the fonts for a beautiful medley of letters. Try placing a word or two in your collage and highlight it with a specific paint or just let it sit in the background waiting to be discovered. Change things up by using just the characters or symbols. How cool would an album cover look covered in all ampersands?

# miscellany layers

One embellishment on a page looks so lonely. Why not group them to make a statement? I love adding sticker letters, chipboard and buttons all in one grouping. With this simple technique, you will be able to add embellishments to your layout with ease.

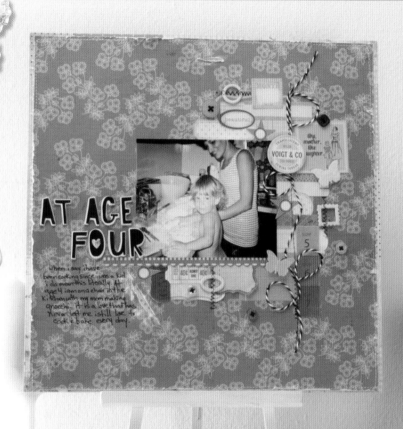

## AT AGE 4

I was giggling when I found this photo among the old slides my dad brought me. Could this picture be any more 1970s? I asked my mom if the refrigerator was avocado green but she told me, "No, but the stove and the walls were." My mom and I still cook together sometimes. In fact, she was coming over the day that I made this layout to make gnocchi with me.

The patterned paper is torn around the edges to show another layer of patchwork patterned paper. See **Lovely** on page 22.

Supplies: alphabet, buttons (Cosmo Cricket); chipboard (Maya Road); patterned paper (Lily Bee Designs, The Girls' Paperie); pen (Sakura Identi Pen); stickers (Crate Paper, Jenni Bowlin, Studio Calico); twine (The Twinery)

## TEA-RRIFIC **CARD**

I love tea—I mean **love** tea—so it's no surprise I would create such a tea-rrific card. I started by creating a layer of buttons on the background. Once I had a pleasant pattern, I removed some of the buttons and added in some pops of pink stickers.

Supplies: cardstock: (Bazzill Basics Paper); chipboard (Maya Road); ink (Ranger Industries); patterned paper (October Afternoon, The Girls' Paperie); stamp (Purple Onion Designs); stickers (Crate Paper); other: vintage buttons

Materials: patterned paper, variety of label and shaped stickers, scalloped chipboard pieces, buttons, sewing machine and thread, twine, pop-up adhesive

1 Start this piece by gathering some of your favorite embellishments and pieces to work with.

2 Begin by randomly placing label stickers down the right side of the page. Then add another layer of label stickers, overlapping the first layer slightly. Keep repeating this process until you have built up a background of label and shaped stickers on the right side of the patterned paper page.

3 Next, add some randomly placed chipboard pieces to the layers of stickers and machine-stitch using a zigzag stitch. Then, add some randomly placed buttons to the layers of stickers and chipboard pieces and stitch in place. Add a meandering piece of twine over the layers and stitch in place. See **Meandering Twine** on page 42.

4 Finally, add one more label sticker using a pop-up adhesive to complete the label collage.

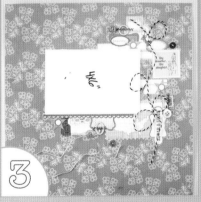

## more layers

Gather up some of your beloved pieces, like rub-ons, buttons, bling, flowers, stamps and stickers. Then, work in a small concentrated area or cover the whole page. A cool trick you can use is tossing buttons or flowers up in the air and see where they fall.

# stacked and stitched titles

I love playing around with fonts, mixing them up, combining two or three of them. With this technique, you will be mixing two different fonts to create a beautiful stacked title, adding flair to your creations.

### BOYS OF SUMMER

In the beginning, this layout was mostly greens, blues, browns and yellows, but it felt like it was missing something. I inserted the pops of red in little doses. It was the perfect color to add a little bit of flair to this page. Notice how I placed the red in a visual triangle around the page to create flow.

I love adding strips of patterned paper to the top and bottoms of my layout for added interest. Sometimes I use border punches to create another layer. See **Magical** on page 20.

Supplies: alphabet (Jillibean Soup, BasicGrey); fabric strip, stickers, wooden embellishments (Studio Calico); paint (Ranger Industries); patterned paper (Lily Bee Designs, Crate Paper); patterned paper, stickers (Jenni Bowlin); patterned paper (Crate Paper); pen (Sakura Identi Pen); pin (Maya Road)

Materials: patterned paper, sewing machine and thread, cardstock letters in two sizes

1 Using a sewing machine, straight stitch following the lines of the patterned paper.

2 Using a sewing machine, straight stitch through the title to give it more texture. It is also a quick way to secure the title.

3 Using the smaller of the cardstock letters, layer and adhere (or straight stitch) the beginning title (or subtitle) to the larger cardstock letters.

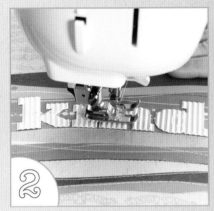

## odds & ends

This technique is a great way to use up scraps of alphabets in a playful way. You can mix and match colors and font styles to create a spunky title. Want something a bit more vintage? Try using cream, white or brown colored alphabets, mixing up the fonts and sanding the edges to antique them a bit. Then, stack the letters on top of each other and stitch them down to complete the look.

# tucking in embellishments

I love looking for spaces here and there to tuck in an embellishment. By using lots of layers of patterned paper, fabric, etc., I find the perfect spots to slip in a label, button or chipboard accent.

## READY TO FLY

It seems like just yesterday I was walking Lexi to kindergarten on the first day of school. I should have known this day would come quickly when, at the beginning of the second week, she turned to me, hands in the air like a stop sign, to tell me she could walk herself to her classroom. Always an independent girl, I know she really is ready to fly.

Supplies: alphabet, chipboard, patterned paper (Lily Bee Designs); brads (Crate Paper); chipboard, flower, trim (Maya Road); player piano paper (Etsy Kenner Road); punch (EK Success, Martha Stewart Crafts); sticker (Jenni Bowlin); other: vintage buttons

## SWEET FRIEND **CARD**

I really love how this card shows the crossover between the categories of scrapbooking, papercraft and mixed-media. After completing a sewing project, I had some scraps of fabric left over that I knew would make a perfect card. I tucked some zipper trim and border stickers into the fabric and stitched it all down. It's fun and unexpected to tuck in sewing notions.

Supplies: brads (Making Memories); cardstock (Bazzill Basics Paper); doily (Martha Stewart Crafts); fabric (Amy Butler); flower (Sassafras Lass); stickers (October Afternoon, Crate Paper); trim (Maya Road)

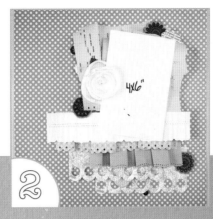

Materials: patterned paper, punches, vintage paper, flowers, buttons, brads, chipboard pieces

1 On the background paper, adhere strips of punched patterned paper making sure only to adhere it in small places to create pockets of space. Next, add layers of vintage papers adhering only at the bottom of the paper so you have areas to add in embellishments.

2 Start tucking in embellishments in the various pockets of space like the flower to the left side. Add in buttons, both under and on top of these pockets, adhering or stitching them into place.

3 Layer buttons on top of chipboard pieces and tuck these into various places on the page.

4 Once you have found a happy placement, adhere the pieces and add in brads. Gluing at the end is great for rearranging those pieces that just aren't quite right.

## loving layers

A good design rule is to always add embellishments in odd numbers. Three is a great number for larger pieces, five or seven for the smaller bits, like bling or brads. Also, remember to try to keep things in a visual triangle. It helps with the flow of the layout, directing the viewer's eye.

# accented journaling

The heart of my layout is always the stories behind the photos. Document-ing everyday life or my thoughts is important, but I want to do it in a fun, creative way. You can bring your stories to life and grab the reader's attention simply by adding bits of paint, bling, buttons, or brads to those sweet words.

## DORKAPOLIS

This layout all happened thanks to a blog post I shared a while ago. I was out and about doing "mommy errands" when I plopped on my sunglasses. I totally didn't notice one of the eye pieces was missing and couldn't figure out why I was getting crazy looks of disbelief from passersby. I even ordered my Chai tea in those beautiful glasses. After I got home, I looked in the rear view mirror and noticed my silly mistake. I couldn't help but laugh at myself and revel in my complete dorkiness.

Supplies: alphabet (American Crafts); alphabet, embellishments (Cosmo Cricket, Jenni Bowlin, Crate Paper, Lily Bee Designs, Me & My Big Ideas, Maya Road, Prima Marketing Inc., 7 Gypsies, Studio Calico); patterned paper (October Afternoon)

Materials: patterned paper, pencil, ruler, paint, playing card, sewing machine, two threads, buttons, brads, rhinestones, chipboard pieces, black pen

1 Using a pencil and a ruler, draw two vertical lines at 2" (5cm) and 10" (25cm) vertically down to about 9½" (24cm). This will be the area for journaling. Using cream paint and a playing card, scrape paint in a downward motion in the penciled in area creating a backdrop for the elements. Let dry.

2 Next, using a pencil and a ruler, draw in lines approximately ½" (13mm) apart down the vertical space. Using a sewing machine, machine-stitch a straight stitch using light thread on these horizontal lines. Next change out the thread to red and add some random zigzag stitches onto the straight stitches.

3 Place random bits of embellishments on the journaling lines like buttons, rhinestones, brads, etc. To add a bit of whimsy, I placed some patterned paper banners that I had cut out from a larger piece of patterned paper.

4 Finally, journal on these lines as desired.

## the good stuff

This technique is the perfect way to add seemingly random bits to those unique journaling lines. Use contrasting threads for some more excitement like the red thread on this layout. You can hand stitch these journaling lines, adding in different stitches for a whole new look.

# outlined titles

Have you ever come up with the perfect title to find that you don't have enough matching letters to complete it? Or the color is just wrong for the layout but you totally love the font? This technique shows you how to use sticker letters to create your own custom title to make your project really pop.

## THE LADIES

I have been begging my son to let me scrap with these photos. He finally agreed now that this event happened years ago. I am so happy to have this story documented. I wanted the layout to reflect his quirky sense of humor. He never fails to make me laugh with his quick wit and unconventional view of the world.

Supplies: alphabet (Pink Paislee); cardstock (American Crafts); fabric strips, spray ink (Studio Calico); gesso, matte medium, paint (Ranger Industries); patterned paper (October Afternoon); spray ink (Maya Road, Tattered Angels)

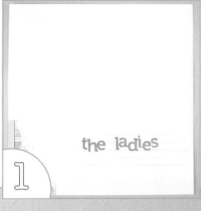

Materials: cardstock, pencil, ruler, ledger paper, letter stickers, pen, two coordinating spray inks, tweezers, eraser

the ladies

**1** Using a pencil and ruler, draw some journaling lines on your page. Next, using letter stickers, add your title to the middle of the journaling lines.

**2** Using spray ink, mist the title from above, letting ink lightly coat the letters. Next, spray a second ink over the first ink and spray closer to the sticker letters.

**3** Using a black pen, outline the title of the page and add journaling.

**4** Carefully remove letter stickers by gently grasping the stickers with tweezers. Erase the penciled-in journaling lines from the title and the journaling.

### snippet

You can get a fine mist on your layouts by holding the spray ink bottles high above the patterned paper. Try sealing the patterned paper with a gel matte medium because it allows you to rub off any excess ink with a paper towel.

Whether rubber stamps or acrylic stamps, I dig them. Why you ask? I am happy to tell you that they add yet another layer to my projects—be it scrapbook or altered items. In many fun shapes and styles, the stamps are an art within themselves. I stroll the store aisles looking for the perfect image to complete a page. I have open shelves with many stamps stacked in plain view inspiring me to create. Sometimes they whisper to me, "Play with me, create with me." I love the potential they hold and the images they can become once used in the perfect spot.

# ✳ art of staMps

I admit I used to be a little scared of them and only used them on cards. What if I don't like how it turns out on my page? What if I mess up the image? It's so permanent. Then I discovered ways around those "what ifs." You can stamp the image on a scrap sheet of paper, cut it out and adhere it on the page you want to accent. Also, if you don't like the placement on the page, cover it up. I like using them in unconventional ways, turning them into 3-D embellishments and stamping on the page as a border, repeating the same image over and over again. And that's just the beginning. You can take them to the next level with so many different mediums like clear embossing powder, paints and spray inks. When we let go of the fear and just play around, we open up to a world of creative possibilities.

# stamped borders

I love using stamps on a border to complete a page, and seemingly random stamps can really come together to complement your layout. I like to add in a few surprises, like patterned paper or colored inks. Sometimes I get crazy and use clear embossing powder to add the images on the sides of the page.

## 4 GENTS

I love this photo of my father-in-law, Phil, holding my husband Andrew. I also love seeing Phil's family photo hanging on the wall in the background. I used the photo as my color inspiration for the layout. It has that 1970s feel to it with the vintage-like patterned paper and the "harvest gold" yellow. Take a closer look and you will notice that the number 4 is repeated throughout the layout. Tiny brown paint splatters are sprinkled on the background as well.

Supplies: alphabet (American Crafts); ink, paint, spray ink (Ranger Industries); patterned paper (Crate Paper, Jenni Bowlin); stamps (Purple Onion Designs); stencil (The Crafter's Workshop); tags/tickets (Cocoa Daisy, Staples); thread (DMC); other: buttons, fabric

Materials: patterned paper, stamps, brown ink, acrylic block, scissors, glue

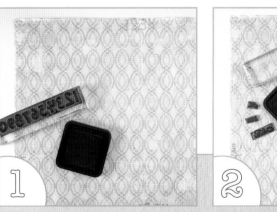

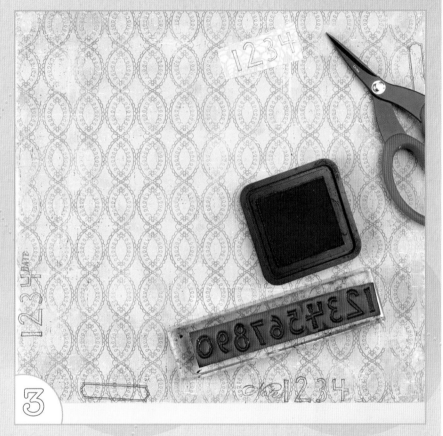

1 Using number stamps and brown ink, stamp on the top center, toward the bottom of the left side, and toward the right, on the bottom of the patterned paper.

2 Using the label stamp and brown ink, stamp near the number stamp on the top, stamp on the bottom near the left side, and on the right side near the top. Fill in these areas using text stamps and brown ink.

3 Using the number stamp and brown ink, stamp numbers on a coordinating piece of patterned paper. Cut out one number of the coordinating stamp of patterned paper inside the stamp lines so none of the stamp shows. Adhere the number to the center of the number stamp already located on the edge of the patterned paper.

4 Cut out bits of wood grain patterned paper and adhere to the center of the stamped labels.

## got stamps?

Don't forget to stamp off the edge of the paper. This technique looks great in a smaller frame on the inside of a layout. Try using a mask stencil and stamps to create a nifty new shape on your layout, be it a bracket, square or circle. Try clear embossing the stamps for a completely different look.

# repetition of stamps

If one beautiful image is good, then three or more is better. I love repeating elements on my pages and look for opportunities to do this with stamps. An open stamp, like a postage stamp or label, is a great way to repeat an element and add in a few more layers.

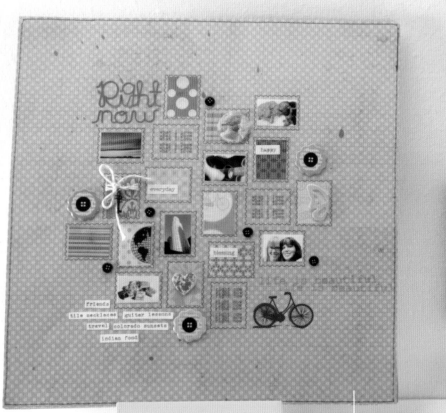

## RIGHT NOW

This layout all started with that postage stamp. It was too cute not to repeat all over the background of my layout. I decided to fill in those openings with pictures of my life right at that particular moment. Think of it as a snapshot of my life. It is a great way to capture a day, week or month of your life.

The rub-on in the stamped rectangles was actually one large phrase. I decided to cut it down into smaller pieces to fit inside the images.

Supplies: alphabet (Studio Calico); brad (Making Memories); chipboard, patterned paper, rub-on, stamps, stickers (Lily Bee Designs); chipboard, spray ink (Maya Road); embellishment (7 Gypsies); ink (Ranger Industries); stickers (The Girls' Paperie); twine (The Twinery); other: fabric tissue

## HELLO **CARD**

This card to me says, "Hello, pull up a chair, and let's chat." I stamped the chair two times on kraft cardstock and then two more times on the yellow patterned paper. I trimmed one of the yellow chair's arms and popped them up using 3-D adhesive to give the last chair more texture.

Supplies: alphabet, fabric strip (Studio Calico); cardstock (Bazzill Basics Paper); ink (Ranger Industries); patterned paper (Pink Paislee, October Afternoon); stamp (Etsy Mothball Charlie) other: 3-D adhesive

**1**

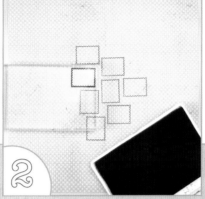

**2**

Materials: two stamps, acrylic
block, black ink, patterned paper,
assorted embellishments

## stamp it out

Try repeating the same stamp over
the entire paper of a project, creating
your own background. You can stamp
them in the same ink or try different
color inks for an added twist.

**3**

1 Starting in the
center of the
page, using black ink,
stamp the postage
image. Working out
from the center,
continue to place
random images of
the postage stamp.

2 Turn the
postage stamp
image horizontal and
stamp some more
images in a random
pattern.

3 Stamp the
bicycle stamp
next to the bottom
right postage stamp.

4 Embellish
the open
stamped image with
patterned paper and
photographs. Finish
the stamp areas
with bits and pieces
of embellishments
including chipboard,
sticker phrases,
tissue flowers and
twine.

**4**

# clear embossed stamps with mists

I love projects that invite you to touch them because they are so rich in texture. With this technique, you build up that cool texture using clear embossing powder, your favorite stamps and some spray ink. It's clearly a very snazzy technique, highlighting the stamped image and the surrounding area.

Supplies: bling (Recollections by Michaels); brad (Crate Paper); canvas, embossing powder (Ranger Industries); cardstock (Bazzill Basics Paper); gesso, Glass Beads, gel medium (Liquitex); metal (The Jewelry Shoppe); pebble (Prima Marketing); pin, spray ink (Maya Road); punch (Martha Stewart Crafts); stamp (Purple Onion Designs); stencil (The Crafter's Workshop); trim (Crate Paper, Etsy Kenner Road); watercolor paper (Strathmore)

## I SEE MY FRIEND

Have you ever had a friend you could tell all your secrets to? All your wishes, hopes and fears? That's my Martha. I look to her for strength, for understanding, for faith, for hope. She has been my constant companion for many years, one whom I love dearly. She is my role model, but more importantly, my friend.

This is one of those layouts that encompasses so many techniques that are found in this book. Did you notice the transparency flowers? See **Great Love Canvas** on page 28. All the embellishments tucked in here and there? See **Ready to Fly** on page 72. The drips of mists? See **The Boy in the Bucket** on page 120. Or the tissue flowers? See **Sewing Trinket Box** on page 24.

Supplies: alphabet (October Afternoon, Cosmo Cricket); bling (Prima Marketing); brads, metal embellishments (Making Memories); brads (My Mind's Eye); cardstock (American Crafts); chipboard (Fancy Pants Designs); embossing powder, ink (Ranger Industries); flower, rub-on, spray ink (Studio Calico); ink, patterned paper, stickers (Jenni Bowlin); metal embellishments (Tim Holtz); pin, spray ink (Maya Road); rub-on, transparency (Hambly Screenprints); spray mist (Tattered Angels); stamps (Purple Onion Designs); stickers (Pink Paislee); twine (The Twinery)

## SPRING PLAY **TAG**

This cute spring tag started with a layer of gesso over a stencil. I then stamped the circles and dandelion over the background using clear ink and clear embossing powder. Next, I used some spray inks and a paintbrush to create the watercolor background, wiping off the excess inks from the stamped images. If I wanted an area a bit darker, I just added in a touch more mist. I played and played until the tag was just right.

Materials: background cardstock paper, butterfly stamp, acrylic block, yellow ink pad, damask stamp, clear ink, Clear UTEE, heat gun, spray mists, cloth

1 Stamp butterfly images on the background cardstock paper in a random pattern.

2 Next using a large damask stamp and clear embossing ink, stamp the damask stamp over the butterflies on the center of the page. Working quickly, repeat this stamp image again with the clear embossing ink. Sprinkle the embossing ink with Clear UTEE and heat set the embossing powder.

3 Spray the clear image with one or more spray mists, misting from high and low heights. This will allow the mists to vary in size.

4 Dab the excess mist off the embossed stamps for added texture, and to allow easier drying.

## clearly more to note

Try spraying your background with mists before stamping your image. You could stamp partially in the sprayed area and in the plain background. Then, when you spray the embossed image with a second mist, you will have some of the first color peeking through the clear embossed area.

# 3-D stamped images

I totally dig stamped images, but sometimes I want them to be viewed as more than just part of the background. When you stamp multiples of the same image, you can cut out certain details in the images to make your stamps pop more and become the focus of your project.

## BEAUTY **CANVAS**

I had only a rough idea of what I wanted the finished canvas to look like, but I knew I wanted something fairylike. I wanted a lot of texture, so I began building up the background with molding paste, cheesecloth and book paper. While the molding paste was still drying, I used a plastic coffee cup lid to create the ring patterns and added the metal embellishments. Next, I painted the background using a combination of paints and spray inks. The best thing about these two mediums is if you don't like the outcome, you can paint right over it. I added the butterflies and the quote and finished the canvas with some beeswax. I dripped the beeswax down the left edge by using a melting pot. You can create a lot of texture in the background by adding those bits of leftover embellishments into the molding paste.

Supplies: beeswax, gesso, paint (Ranger Industries); canvas (The Artist's Loft by Michaels); metal embellishments (Tim Holtz); molding paste, paint (Golden Artist Colors); spray ink (Maya Road, Tattered Angels); stamp (Purple Onion Designs); other: book paper, cheesecloth

1

2 3

4

Materials: watercolor paper, butterfly stamps, paintbrushes, black ink, palette, spray ink, water, acrylic block, scissors, pop-up adhesive, glitter glue

1 Using permanent black ink, stamp two butterfly images on watercolor paper.

2 Using a palette, pour a little spray ink into a well and add a touch of water. Using paintbrushes and a variety of colors, paint the two butterflies exactly the same.

3 Cut out the first butterfly from the watercolor paper and set it aside. Cut out the second butterfly's center area and add pop-up adhesive. Accent the background butterfly with glitter glue and let it dry.

4 Curl the butterfly's wings using the paintbrush to create a 3-D effect.

## go big

Add this technique with the **Repetition of Stamps** technique (see page 82) and you got one stellar creation. First cover the background paper of your project. Then stamp a couple more images on the same background paper and cut them out. Pop a few of them up on the background page to create a dynamic piece of art!

## IMAGINE **TYPECASE DRAWER**

This typecase drawer developed from the "Imagine" quote stamp. I wanted this home decor piece to be uplifting and a reminder to take a leap and chase down your dreams. In order to bring all the colors together, I used my favorite walnut stain distress ink on all the patterned papers. There are many different stamped images in this piece with some of the elements popped up to stand out a bit more. I can't wait to hang this up in my house!

Supplies: apothecary jars (Tim Holtz); bling (Me & My Big Ideas); brads (BasicGrey, Making Memories); chipboard (Crate Paper); ink (Ranger Industries); metal embellishments (Tim Holtz); patterned paper (Cosmo Cricket, Crate Paper, Jenni Bowlin, October Afternoon); punch (Martha Stewart Crafts); spray ink (Maya Road); stamps (Purple Onion Designs, Cocoa Daisy, Tim Holtz); stickers (7 Gyspies, Jenni Bowlin, October Afternoon, Studio Calico); trim (May Arts); twine (The Twinery); knob, typecase drawer (7 Gyspies); watercolor paper (Strathmore)

istress
nk
abby shutters
Create an aged look on paper
fibers, photos & more
POST CARD

# sprayed ink stamps

I love spray inks. I love stamps. I love spray inks, plus stamps. I was playing around one day and decided to try stamping with spray inks and I got this cool watercolor effect and was hooked. There are so many possibilities with this watercolor effect—have fun playing!

## OH, HAPPY DAY

Oh, happy day indeed! My family has been blessed to spend so much time with my sweet nephew. I am always ready with my camera to capture his sweet looks, especially at his birthday parties. This year he was extra cute as he sang "Happy Birthday" to himself.

Supplies: cardstock (Bazzill Basics Paper); chipboard, spray inks (Maya Road); embossing powder, spray inks (Ranger Industries); gesso (Golden Artist Colors); patterned paper, stickers (October Afternoon); spray inks (Studio Calico); stamp (Purple Onion Designs)

## LOVE **CARD**

Love is universal. Therefore, this card can be used for a wedding gift card, a new baby card, or for just a note of love. I like to have a multi-purpose card in my stash to hand out at a moment's notice. There are so many different ways to add color to naked chipboard. For the chipboard word "love," I took an ink pad and brushed it over the piece until I had the color I wanted.

Supplies: cardstock (Bazzill Basics Paper); chipboard (Maya Road); ink, paint (Ranger Industries); patterned paper (The Girls' Paperie, My Mind's Eye); spray ink (Maya Road, Tattered Angels); stamp (Purple Onion Designs); trim (Etsy Kenner Road)

Materials: script stamp, spray inks, white cardstock, alphabet stamp, scissors

1 Using the script stamp, lay the stamp down with the image side up and spray with multiple colors of spray ink. Stamp the script down on the white cardstock in a random pattern without re-inking the stamp.

2 Using the alphabet stamp, lay the stamp down with the image side up and spray multiple colors of spray ink. Stamp the alphabet stamp down on the white cardstock over the script stamped image.

3 Using scissors, cut the alphabet images into strips and adhere to the background.

## be bold

I stamped the images on a separate cardstock and then added them to my page. Once you feel comfortable with this technique, dare to use it on the background of a page. Be mindful when choosing spray ink colors to use on your stamps because complementary colors will turn a muddy color. Another great option is to spray a nonstick craft mat with mists and dip your stamps into the wet inks.

# stamped titles

There are so many great alphabet stamps out there to use in your projects. You can find both positive and negative image stamps, in other words, stamps that have a complete image and ones that have open space. Each type brings something special to your project. I happen to have a love for alphabet stamps and know that sometimes stamping directly on a layout can be intimidating. Try this technique to add the perfect layered title, without the stress of a miss-step.

## LEARNING TO LOVE

I fully admit that sometimes I still struggle with my self-esteem. It is all too easy for me to slip back into self-doubt and self-sabotage mode. I have learned to stop and take breaks when I am feeling this way. Just the simple act of deep breaths to calm myself.

I really like adding gesso to my layouts to create more texture. I also added some words and paint splatters to the background. Did you notice the reverse embossed circles, too? Or the punched photo that I stitched to the page? For more inspiration see **Complements** on page 118, **The Butterfly Effect** on page 18, **The Boy in the Bucket** on page 120 or the **ATC Cards** on page 60.

Supplies: chipboard (Lily Bee Designs); flower (Studio Calico); gesso, gloss medium, ink, paint (Ranger Industries); patterned paper (Cosmo Cricket); punch (EK Success); rub-on (Hambly Screenprints); rub-on, sticker (Jenni Bowlin); rub-on, spray ink (Maya Road); thread (DMC); twine (The Twinery); other: buttons

Materials: alphabet stamps, acrylic block, black ink, patterned paper, scissors, Glossy Accents Clear Gloss Medium

1 Using black ink and an alphabet stamp, stamp your title on the patterned paper.

2 Using sharp scissors, cut out your title just outside the black edge of the letter.

3 Fill in the center of the stamped image using Glossy Accents Clear Gloss Medium.

## fountain of fonts

Alphabets come in all shapes and sizes, including both open face fonts and closed fonts, each bringing something special to your projects. Try adding some bling or rub-ons to the stamp images before adding the clear glue. Try mixing up the fonts for a playful title.

# watercolored background with inks

Inks make a great background, especially when you use a non-stick craft mat and water to create a watercolor effect. I like using resist fluid to doodle images or words on my backgrounds before adding the inks. This technique is so playful and creates such a movement reminiscent of beautiful watercolor paintings.

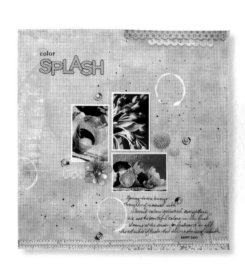

## COLOR SPLASH

There are some cardstocks and patterned papers available that come with glossy accents. These are great to use with this watercolor ink-resist technique because the images are already on the page. I used my pictures as color inspiration for my background. For added color, I also wet the inks with some similar colored mists.

Supplies: alphabet, sticker (October Afternoon); brads (BasicGrey); flowers (Petaloo, Prima Marketing); inks (Ranger Industries); paint (Ranger Industries, Golden Artist Colors); patterned paper (Pink Paislee, Jenni Bowlin, Sassafras Lass, My Mind's Eye); pen (Sakura Identi Pen); punch (Fiskars); rub-ons (Jenni Bowlin, Maya Road)

## CLICK CLICK

One of the moments that clicked for me was the moment I clicked. I found art through photography and saw such beautiful images through the lens. I always have my camera near me, ready to capture life. My family knows and expects it at all events. The kids tell their friends, "She takes lots of pictures so be prepared." It is more of an appendage than a piece of equipment.

Supplies: alphabet, cardstock (American Crafts); fabric strips, wooden embellishments (Studio Calico); inks (Jenni Bowlin); inks, nonstick craft mat (Ranger Industries); Resist Fluid (Maya Road); stamp (Purple Onion Design); thread (DMC)

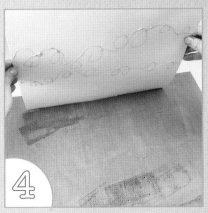

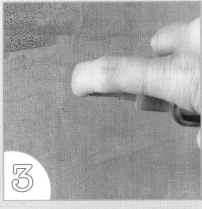

Materials: cardstock, Maya Road Resist Fluid, nonstick craft mat, multiple inks, water mister

1 Using Maya Road Resist Fluid, gently squeeze the fluid medium to create a doodled line across the page from left to right. Let it dry.

2 Using a nonstick craft mat, take a red ink pad and press hard in the bottom left corner of the craft mat. Repeat inking the nonstick craft mat with many colored inks until you cover the background.

3 Using a bottle full of water, spray the craft mat until beads of water appear all over the background.

4 Take a 12"×12" (30cm×30cm) piece of white cardstock and, turning it over, place it on the wet inks, pressing gently all around the page to pick up the ink for a watercolor effect.

5 Using your finger, peel back the resist doodle line to reveal an ink-free doodled line.

## the sweet stuff

Try using a paper piercer and pierce holes along the doodle line about ¼" (6mm) apart. Next, using a needle and floss, backstitch along the pierced line, creating a stitched accent layer. Don't have a craft mat? Try using wax paper; it achieves the same water-resistant effect. I confess, I have a love for rainbow order, colors in perfect harmony. I organize my clothes, my scrapbook and art supplies, and yes, even my threads in rainbow order. I even tried to talk my husband into letting me organize our books in rainbow order.

# stamped layers

Looking for that perfect embellishment but just can't seem to find it? Create it yourself with some stamps, die cut shapes, punches and a button or two. You can create the ideal accent for your project simply by combining layers of items already at your fingertips.

## ALL

You always think as a parent, "Did I do enough for them?" They are growing up into such wonderful people that I have to believe that I did do enough. This layout reminds me of when they were younger. My husband and I would read to them every night, sometimes chapters from longer books and sometimes entire shorter books. They still recall their favorite books and all the voices I had created while reading them. When they relive these moments, it lets me know we did alright as parents.

You can add meaning to your layouts by your choice of embellishments. The nursery rhyme paper echoes the days I would read to my kids. The numbers 1 and 2 have dual meanings—two kids and "one, two, buckle my shoes."

Supplies: alphabet (American Crafts); button, chipboard (Crate Paper); die cuts (Cosmo Cricket); doilies, punch (Martha Stewart Crafts); ink, paint, Embossing Pearl Powder (Ranger Industries); patterned paper (Crate Paper, Lily Bee Designs, October Afternoon); pen (Sakura Identi Pen); stamp (Purple Onion Designs); water-based paint (Shimmerz Paints)

Materials: paper doilies, ink pad—clear and black, blue Embossing Pearl Powder, paintbrush, script stamp, 1" (3cm) and ¾" (19mm) circle punch, dictionary paper, patterned paper, buttons, paper piercer, needle and thread

1 First stamp a paper doily with the clear ink pad. (This will allow the blue Embossing Pearl Powder to stick to the paper better.) Brush the powder over the doily with a paintbrush.

2 Push your script stamp into the black ink pad and stamp the doily.

3 Using your 1" (3cm) circle punch, punch a few circles out of dictionary paper. To add even more of a contrast, rub the edge of the dictionary paper circle in the black ink pad.

4 Build your stamped layer embellishment by placing the dictionary punch onto the stamped doily. To add a bit of whimsy, add a ¾" (19mm) patterned paper circle on top of the dictionary circle. For the final touch, choose a button to complement the rest of the pieces. Using a paper piercer, punch through all the layers, through the top of the button holes. With your needle and coordinating thread, sew all the pieces together through your button holes.

## layer it on

Break out your acrylics, watercolors, spray inks, stamp inks, etc., to color in your background. Try using the clear embossing technique first, before adding in the layer of color. This technique makes a great family craft day. Gather up all the supplies and have fun with the kiddos as they create the fun, fabulous embellishments for your pages.

# alcohol inks

Need a way to dress up those metal accents? Grab your alcohol inks and watch those plain metal embellishments turn into something special right before your eyes. Shabby them up with some brown inks, or go bold with that perfect pop of color to accentuate your designs.

## WE LAUGH

I met my friend Jessi through the Internet. We bonded not only over scrapbooking but over the many similarities in our lives and personalities. We keep in touch through text messages, instant messages and by chatting on the phone. And always, at some point during our conversation, we laugh at something silly that was said, or a goofy thing we did. I love those little moments in our friendship.

For more ideas about using alcohol inks, see **Right Now** on page 82. For directions for making tissue paper flowers, see page 25 and see the **Sewing Trinket Box** on page 24 for a suggestion for using tissue flowers.

Supplies: alcohol ink, ink (Ranger Industries); alphabet (American Crafts); canvas tags, metal clip, ribbon tape (BasicGrey); envelope (Maya Road); metal numbers (Tim Holtz); patterned paper (BasicGrey, Cosmo Cricket); stamp (Cocoa Daisy) sticker, tags (7 Gypsies); thread (DMC)

Materials: nonstick craft mat, metal number, two alcohol inks, tweezers, heat gun

1 On the nonstick craft mat, place a metal number and drip a couple drops of alcohol ink.

2 Using a second alcohol ink, drip a couple more drops onto the metal number layering over the first ink.

3 Using the tweezers to hold the metal number in place, use the heat gun to push the alcohol ink around creating a marble texture. Add more ink as necessary creating a marble texture you like.

## kick it up

Not happy with some areas on your pieces? No problem. Simply dip a cotton swab into some alcohol and gently wipe off the excess. Try this technique on some of your jewelry pieces that need updating. Alcohol inks will also add that bit of color to your transparency shapes.

**5**

There is something so freeing about getting messy with art mediums. It is something that I have loved since I was a little girl in my favorite art class, and that love has never left me.

Paints and inks makes me happy, I mean really happy. There are so many colors and options for different techniques. I have plenty of brushes, but my favorite applicator is my fingers. I call it a good day when I have ink under my fingernails or dried paint on my hands (and thankfully those days happen quite frequently).

I use and love these messy mediums so much that I feel my layouts and projects seem naked without a bit of splatter or bits of drips on the page. I usually start my layouts with a picture or story in mind, and follow it up with a choice of ink, paint or both to complement my layout.

There are a lot of ways to play with paints and inks on your projects—from premade stencils, to homemade masks using punches and die cuts. Fluid resist mediums and gesso also add to the fun of paints and mists, making your options even greater. And remember, you don't have to be an expert to play with these techniques, you just need a willingness to get a little messy!

*✳ art of messy*

# stencils

Want to take your spray inks and mists to the next level? Grab some stencils (or masks) and let the fun begin. Many manufactures have released so many cool designs and shapes to add a bit of drama to your pages. The best part is you can change them up with just a sheet of cardstock paper. So grab those mists and stencils and let's play.

## ADHD

I used both premade stencils and a homemade mask on this layout. Once I decided to spray the circles, I didn't want to cover the entire background with that stencil, so I cut the center out of a piece of cardstock leaving a few inches to frame the outside edge of the circle stencil. After spraying the numbers stencil, I purposely placed the cloud rub-ons upside down to create a different shape. For this layout, I wanted to emulate Anthony's ADHD with my erratic build up and placement of layers.

Supplies: alphabet (Jillibean Soup); cardstock (Bazzill Basic Paper); fabric strip, patterned paper, rub-ons (Studio Calico); pen (Sakura Identi Pen); rub-ons (Hambly Screenprints); rub-ons, spray ink (Maya Road); stencils (The Crafter's Workshop)

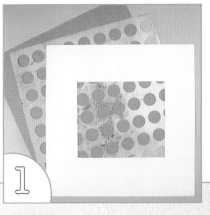

1

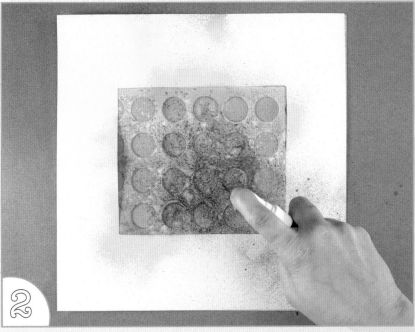

2

3

Materials: cardstock, circle stencil, homemade mask, multiple mists, number stencil

1 Take the cardstock and place the circle stencil on top of the cardstock and add the homemade mask to block out part of the stencil.

2 Spray the circle stencil and homemade mask using the lightest mist first. Spray the circle stencil again using a medium-light mist. Then, spray the circle stencil again with an even darker mist. Let the cardstock dry.

3 Remove the homemade mask and the circle stencil and place the number stencil on the sprayed and dry cardstock. Using leftover cardstock, cover the left part of the number stencil and mist the numbers using a very dark mist.

## get inked

Start your layers of spray ink from lightest to darkest so you have a better handle on the coverage of your mists and the value of your colors. Use a piece of cardstock to cover up the edges of the stencil before spraying. You will have the start of another layout with a groovy misted edge.
Cut small pieces of cardstock and spray your mists on each sheet. Label each piece with the manufacturer and color. Punch a hole in the upper left corner and place on a binder ring. That way, when you want to spray a layout, you can pull out your spray swatches to get the perfect color for your project.

## LIFE ATC TRAY

Family ties are important. My **Life ATC Tray** was created for my sister-in-law and her family. I started with a collection of coordinating patterned papers and stickers. I changed the photos to black and white to make them pop against the white tray. The last touches I added were the little embellishments and stickers. All of the little cards were machine-stitched before I adhered them into the tray.

Supplies: alphabet (Jillibean Soup); ATC tray (7 Gypsies); canvas, envelope, chipboard, trim, labels (Maya Road); clear embossing powder, paint (Ranger Industries); embellishment (Jenni Bowlin); flowers (Prima Marketing); glass bottle, metal embellishment (Tim Holtz); patterned paper (Crate Paper, October Afternoon, My Mind's Eye, Lily Bee Designs); pin (Little Yellow Bicycle); spray ink (Maya Road, Tattered Angels); stencil (The Crafter's Workshop); stickers (Crate Paper); tag (K & Company); twine (The Twinery)

# punches as masks

Using your punched out paper is a great way to create homemade masks. You can use one punch shape or multiple punch shapes to create your own unique look. Die cuts can also be used for this technique, making the possibilities even more endless.

## TREE OF LIFE

Made of quartz, and etched on both sides, I was captivated by the beauty of this necklace that I found in a little jewelry shop in Mykonos, Greece. When the shop owner told me the story behind the etched art, "The Tree of Life," I was sold, knowing how much of my life this small necklace represented.

Supplies: alphabet, spray ink (Studio Calico); cardstock (Bazzill Basics Paper); patterned paper (October Afternoon, Hambly Screenprints, Lily Bee Designs); pen (Sakura Identi Pen); punch (Martha Stewart Crafts); spray ink (Maya Road, Tattered Angels)

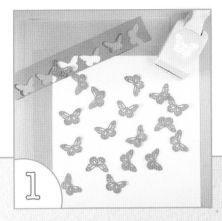

1

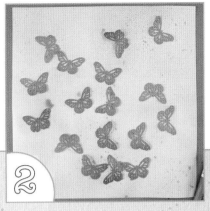

2

3

## punch it up

If you want your spray ink backgrounds to be even more consistent, you can use a brayer immediately after spraying to spread the ink evenly. Another idea for this technique is to spray with one ink and then add more of the punches before spritzing with another ink.

4

Materials: plain cardstock, butterfly punch, white cardstock, yellow, blue and gray mist

1 Using a butterfly punch and the plain cardstock, punch out multiple butterflies. Take your butterfly punches and scatter them across the white cardstock, overlapping a few of them.

2 Take the yellow mist and spray the upper right, upper left and bottom left of the white cardstock. Using the blue mist, spray between the yellow mist. It is OK if the mists overlap a little bit.

3 Next, take the gray mist and mist from high above the cardstock so it adds light mist layer.

4 Remove the butterfly punches and place them in a bag that zips to keep and reuse for another project.

# make your own stencil

A magnetic punch is an awesome way to make your own stencil because, with the magnetic mechanisms, you can place the punch anywhere. You can also achieve this look by using die cuts, or punched pieces, and cutting around them.

## MUSTACHE LOVE

I loved Paolo before the mustache, but I might love him just a little bit more because of the mustache. He is such a genuine person who radiates warmth and love. Christine and I had a blast walking around the convention center with him—laughing the entire time. And when we spotted those mustache props, we knew we had the perfect photo-op.

The seam binding is another great example of meandering ribbon like **Off Centered** found of page 42. The binding likes to curl, so I tacked it down with bits of liquid adhesive.

Supplies: alphabet (Jenni Bowlin); button, patterned paper (The Girls' Paperie); chipboard, spray ink, tags (Maya Road); ink (Ranger Industries); patterned paper (October Afternoon); pen (American Crafts); punch (EK Success, Martha Stewart Crafts); spray ink (Tattered Angels); thread (DMC); transparency (Hambly Screenprints); trim (Etsy Kenner Road)

1

2

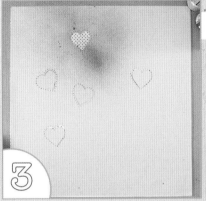

3

## stencil me in

If you want the inked hearts to be the focus, use only one strand of the thread to stitch around the images. Choose a patterned paper that has a quilted style to add a bit more texture. You can use leftover chipboard to create stencils, too. Simply trace around the shapes and cut them out using a craft knife.

Materials: cardstock, magnetic heart punch, patterned paper, multiple mists, paper piercer, needle and thread

1 Using a magnetic heart punch, punch out five heart shapes in a random pattern on the cardstock—saving the hearts that are punched out.

2 Next, place your punched-out cardstock over the patterned paper and cover up four of the five hearts.

3 Spray the first heart and let it dry. Repeat this step using the punched-out heart shapes to cover every heart except the one you are working on. For a more playful effect, spray each heart a different color.

4 Using a paper piercer, punch holes around the misted heart shape. Using a needle and three strands of color-coordinating thread, backstitch around each heart.

4

# using household items as stencils

I am always on the hunt for new items to use as masks or stencils. Bubble wrap is a great, inexpensive item to use with your mists. Punchinella (sequin waste) is another item I like to keep on hand to use with spray inks. Look around your house for those fun, little items that will create movement and texture on your projects.

## SOAK IT ALL IN **CANVAS TRIO**

One of my favorite papercrafts to make are these little altered canvases. I usually do them in groups of three and pick a theme for the grouping. I love that I can use all kinds of mixed-media and scrapbook supplies on them. This canvas trio is about my love for bubble baths. Nothing relaxes me more than reading a good book or magazine while taking a dip in my bathtub.

Supplies: bling (Me & My Big Ideas); brad (Making Memories); canvas (Artist's Loft) gesso (Liquitex); glitter (Martha Stewart Crafts); ink (Ranger Industries); paints (Ranger Industries, Liquitex); patterned paper (The Girls' Paperie); rub-ons (Lily Bee Designs); spray ink (Maya Mists); stamps (Purple Onion Designs); trim (The Girls' Paperie); other: book paper, wooden skewer, Punchinella, bubble wrap

## 1 WEEK

I like saving leftover alphabets and lace paper to use as stencils for my layouts. There are so many cool fonts and shapes that it makes me giddy with excitement. I have a canvas tote on my shelves that holds these little extra beauties.

Supplies: alphabet, cardstock (American Crafts); die-cut flower (Sassafras Lass); lace paper (KI Memories); patterned paper (My Mind's Eye, Sassafras Lass, BasicGrey, Studio Calico); punch (Fiskars); spray inks (Maya Road, Studio Calico); stickers (Sassafras Lass); thread (DMC); trim (Cocoa Daisy); other: burlap, chipboard alphabet leftovers

Materials: mini canvas, foam brush, gesso, book paper, palette, paints, paintbrush, acrylic paint, mists, bubble wrap, Punchinella (sequin waste)

1 Using a foam brush, spread the gesso over the canvas to give it texture. Add old book papers on top of the gesso and smooth them with the foam brush.

2 Using your favorite paints and paintbrushes, paint the background of the canvas and let it dry. Add another paint color to your canvas. (I also flicked a little paint for some texture.)

3 Using a complementary mist, spray the bubble wrap and stamp it on the canvas.

4 Take the Punchinella and place it over the canvas and spray mist on the canvas to create another layer.

## foundations

Building up layers takes time, but it is the journey of creating that I enjoy the most. Often, I will start a piece with gesso and text. While the gesso is drying, I will go work on another project. I tend to have multiple projects in various stages around my craft room.

# misted titles

Using a fluid medium to create doodles and words on my page makes me feel like I am back in school doodling all over my notebooks. This is a simple yet effective technique that can really add impact to your layout.

## AUTHENTIC

I guess you could call me "unconventional." I like creating holiday layouts that entice the reader to take a closer look to find out the layouts are seasonal. This Valentine's Day layout started with my photos and the resist fluid phrases. If you were in my studio that day, you would have heard me giggling with excitement. Creative play makes me so happy, and I felt like a kid discovering something while working on this layout.

Supplies: cardstock (Bazzill Basics Paper); ink (Ranger Industries); patterned paper (Lily Bee Designs); patterned paper, transparency (Hambly Screenprints); pen (Sakura Identi Pen); punches (EK Success, Fiskars); resist fluid, spray ink (Maya Road); stamp (Cocoa Daisy); staples (Tim Holtz); sticker (7 Gypsies); twine (The Twinery); other: buttons

## THANKS **CARD**

I had this leftover sprayed-ink stamped image from when I created the **Love Card** on page 90. It was so pretty and begged to be used. I decided to use the color as inspiration for this card. I wrote out the word thanks a couple times on a piece of cardstock until I found the right size and shape. After the resist fluid was dry, I sprayed the "thanks" with three different mists.

Supplies: cardstock (American Crafts, Bazzill Basics Paper); patterned paper (October Afternoon, Lily Bee Designs); resist fluid (Maya Road); spray ink (Maya Road, Tattered Angels); stamp (Purple Onion Designs); trim (Stampin' Up!)

Materials: cardstock, Maya Road Resist Fluid, acrylic coffee ring stamp, brown mist, ink

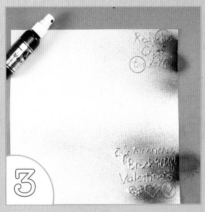

1 Starting at the top right side, gently squeeze the resist, writing out words that describe the story of the layout. Continue writing words down the right side of the page until you have your desired effect. Once the resist is dry, it changes color to a blue hue.

2 Next, using an acrylic stamp and ink, stamp the image over the words in various spots.

3 After shaking up the brown mist, spray the mist, covering up the resist words.

4 Let the mist dry and, then, using your fingers, gently peel away the resist (carefully) from the cardstock.

## mystified?

Not comfortable writing right out of the bottle? Use a pencil to draw out your titles first and then go over the lines with the resist fluid. After you have misted and pulled away the resist, simply erase the text with a good white eraser. Practice makes perfect. Use your scraps to practice your doodles. If you like the end results, you can add them to any project.

# layers of paint

It is amazing to me how a few bits of paint can transform a layout. Whether you are scraping it down the page, sponging it on using a homemade stencil or dripping it across the page, playing with paint brings your projects to life in such a unique way. Get ready to get a little messy and add splashes of color and texture to your layouts.

## SO HARD

This layout is great for showing many layers of paint, but did you notice the other layers? There are stamped images around the borders of the layout, similar to the ones found on **Stamped Borders** on page 80. I layered a sticker, some rub-ons, a journal card and fabric on top of the painted background and then machine-stitched it all together making a cohesive piece. I used a digital frame around my pictures making this layout a hybrid and layering yet another element.

Supplies: alphabet (American Crafts); buttons (Jenni Bowlin); digital frame of stacked photo clusters by Katie Pertiet (Designer Digitals); fabric sticker, patterned paper, journal card (Studio Calico); ink, paint (Ranger Industries); matte medium (Liquitex); patterned paper (Lily Bee Designs); pen (Sakura Identi Pen); rub-ons (Hambly Screenprints); stamp (Purple Onion Designs); staples (Tim Holtz); stickers (October Afternoon); thread (DMC); twine (The Twinery)

Materials: paint palette, patterned paper, black, teal and white paint, matte medium, water, paintbrush, palette knife, foam brush, 3"×12" (8cm×30cm) piece of cardstock, circle punch

1 In a paint palette, mix a lot of white paint and a touch of black paint to make a light gray color. Next, mix a little teal paint with white paint to create a light aqua color. Add a bit of matte medium and water to make the aqua paint a bit translucent. Lastly, mix some white paint and black paint to make a dark gray color. Add a bit of water to make the dark gray paint a little milky.

2 Using a paintbrush, add some of the light gray paint to the edge of the palette knife and scrape down the middle of the page with lots of pressure so the paint spreads thin. Let the paint dry.

3 Using a 3"×12" (8cm×30cm) piece of cardstock and a 1½" (13mm) circle punch, punch a line of circles down the piece of cardstock from the top to the bottom, creating a stencil. Place the stencil approximately 3" (8cm) in from the left. Using a foam brush, dab the aqua paint across the stencil creating the line of circles down the page.

4 Using a round paintbrush, load up the dark gray paint and tap paint onto the patterned paper to create splatters.

## getting messy

I like adding a bit of water and matte medium to my paints so they are a bit translucent. This allows the patterned paper to peek through and add more texture to the layout. Punches are an easy way to make a stencil for a page. Make sure you wash out your paintbrushes right away while you are waiting for the paint to dry. If you are impatient like me, try using a heat gun to dry your background.

## HALLOWEEN TAG **DISPLAY**

It is so much fun to create a seasonal tag display. I made one for winter and decided to make one for Halloween. You can make them with your kids as a great family activity or by yourself, having fun with creative play. And when the season is over, you can take your tags down and create a mini album out of them!

Supplies: acrylic bling (Fiskars Cloud 9 Designs); acrylic die cuts (Fancy Pants Designs); acrylic flowers (Pink Paislee); bingo card, chipboard (Jenni Bowlin); brads (Making Memories); clear embossing powder (Ranger Industries); flowers (Prima Marketing, Maya Road, The Girls' Paperie); gesso (Liquitex, Golden Artist Colors); glass beads, string medium (Liquitex); metal embellishments (Tim Holtz, Teresa Collins Designs, The Jewelry Shoppe); paint (Ranger Industries, Liquitex, Golden Artist Colors); patterned paper (The Girls' Paperie, My Mind's Eye); rub-ons (Maya Road, Studio Calico, Hambly Screenprints); spray ink (Maya Road, Ranger Industries); stamps, tissue tape (Tim Holtz); stencil (The Crafter's Workshop); stickers (The Girls' Paperie); tags (Staples); wooden die cut (Kaisercraft); other: frame, fabric

### tag, you're it!

Tags are a great way to try out techniques. You can try out stencils to get a feel for their shapes, combine colors to see how they look, or see how other tools paint on the tags. If you look closely at this display, you will find a variety of techniques from stencil play, to the layering of embellishments.

# gesso and mists

There is something very pleasing about scraping gesso across my page to add in texture or sometimes to tone down patterns. When the spray inks hit the gesso, they take on a new quality, really retaining that glossy wet look.

## COMPLEMENTS

All the bits and pieces that may not work on their own really come together harmoniously on this layout. For instance, journaling in only a few of the stamped labels, or the lone photo near the top (which is another happy little accident). I was deciding between the two photos and casually tossed the one of my daughter Lexi away, when it landed on the page at that angle. I knew then it was staying on the layout just as it had fallen, and I would build the layers up higher to include it.

Supplies: acrylic, chipboard, pin, spray ink, ticket (Maya Road); acrylic (Fancy Pants Designs); alcohol ink, gesso, ink (Ranger Industries); alphabet, stickers (Jenni Bowlin); chipboard, patterned paper (Lily Bee Designs); filmstrip ribbon (Tim Holtz); patterned paper (Cosmo Cricket); pen (Sakura Identi Pen); spray ink (Studio Calico); stamps (Purple Onion Designs); stencil (The Crafter's Workshop); tag (Staples); twine (The Twinery)

## XOXO **CARD**

This cute card was created by first laying down a layer of gesso and then using a harlequin stencil and pink spray ink. The pink ink took on a red hue on the gesso, which is exactly what I was hoping for. I outlined the Eiffel Tower die cut with a black pen to give it a little more oomph.

Supplies: alphabet (American Crafts); chipboard (Pink Paislee); flowers, trim, pin, spray ink (Maya Road); gesso (Golden Artist Colors); patterned paper (October Afternoon); pen (Sakura Identi Pen); stencil (The Crafter's Workshop)

Materials: patterned paper, acrylic playing card, gesso, bubble wrap, stylus, blue and yellow mists

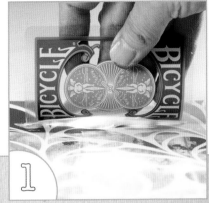

1 Using an acrylic playing card, load up gesso onto the edge and scrape from right to left on the page, working from the top to the bottom of the page.

2 Push a piece of bubble wrap into the gesso while it is still wet to add a new texture and pattern to your page. Keep the bubble wrap in one area of the gesso.

3 In the areas not affected by the bubble wrap, draw words that work with the theme of your layout with a stylus.

4 Once the gesso is dry, lightly mist blue onto the background by spraying the mist from high above (this allows for finer drops). After shaking up the yellow mist, unscrew the mist nozzle and set the mist bottle aside. Using only the nozzle, fling the yellow onto the page creating a drizzled mist pattern onto the patterned paper background.

## written word

Try using other items to create textures in the gesso like plastic wrap, coffee sleeves, or Punchinella (sequin waste). Take a playing card and scratch lines in the gesso or use toys, like Legos, to create cool shapes. Write a single word over and over again. Scared of bold patterned papers? You can easily tone it down with a layer of gesso.

# splatters of paint

Splatters of paint are like sprinkles of goodness dripped across your design, adding texture and color in a beautiful little layer. Using different paintbrushes creates different drips on your backgrounds, changing the page dynamics. Grab your paintbrushes and get a little messy.

## THE BOY IN THE BUCKET

In this technique, I used small pieces of paper to show you how many different types of splatters can be achieved using different brushes. Once you feel more confident flinging a brush across your page, go for the entire background. Just make sure you are wearing clothes you don't mind covering in paint!

Supplies: alphabet (Studio Calico, Cosmo Cricket); bingo number (Maya Road); cardstock (Bazzill Basics Paper); embellishment (Jenni Bowlin); ink, paint (Ranger Industries); sticker (Crate Paper); walnut ink (Tsukineko); punch (EK Success); other: book paper

## APART

I miss my husband every day. We are currently living on different continents because he works as a commercial pilot for a Middle East company. The separation has taught me how much I love and appreciate all the things he does for me and our family.

Using some spray inks, spray into a box to get the ink up into the nozzle. Unscrew the top and spray again with the stem of the nozzle over the page to create a wide splat. Turn the nozzle upside down and pull back the stem with your finger. Let go to create movement splats.

Supplies: alphabet (Studio Calico); buttons, stickers, patterned paper (Cosmo Cricket); envelope (Maya Road); pin (Maya Road); punch (EK Success); rub-on (Jenni Bowlin, Studio Calico); spray ink (Studio Calico, Ranger Industries); thread (DMC)

1

2

3

4

## paint it on

You can find empty spray bottles in your local craft stores or in the beauty travel section of most large department stores. Can't decide on a color for your layout? Neutrals always work, so try adding a black, chocolate brown or white to the layout. Splatters like to travel, so make sure you cover the area you are working on with some scrap paper. Consider wearing play clothes and/or an apron when working with paints.

Materials: cardstock, paper trimmer, white, black, teal and yellow paint, palette, water, matte medium, small round tip paintbrush, toothbrush, square tip paintbrush

1 Using a paper trimmer, cut down a 12"×12" (30cm×30cm) piece of cardstock into 2"×2" (5cm×5cm) squares (optional—round the corners of the 2" [5cm] squares). In a paint palette, mix teal paint with white paint to a light aqua color. Add matte medium and water to make the aqua paint a bit translucent. Also, mix yellow paint with water to thin out the consistency. Finally, mix a light gray with the white and black paints, adding water to thin out the paint.

2 Using a small round brush, load black paint on the brush and then using a quick flick of the wrist, fling paint over a few 2" (5cm) squares. This creates paint splatters in motion. Repeat with the gray paint.

3 Using a toothbrush, load yellow paint onto the bristles. Using your thumb, pull bristles back and let them go over a 2" (5cm) square. This creates small, tiny splatters.

4 Using a large square brush, load the teal paint onto the brush. Take your pointer finger and pull bristles back and let them go over a 2" (5cm) square. This creates a whisker type of paint splatter. Repeat with the aqua paint.

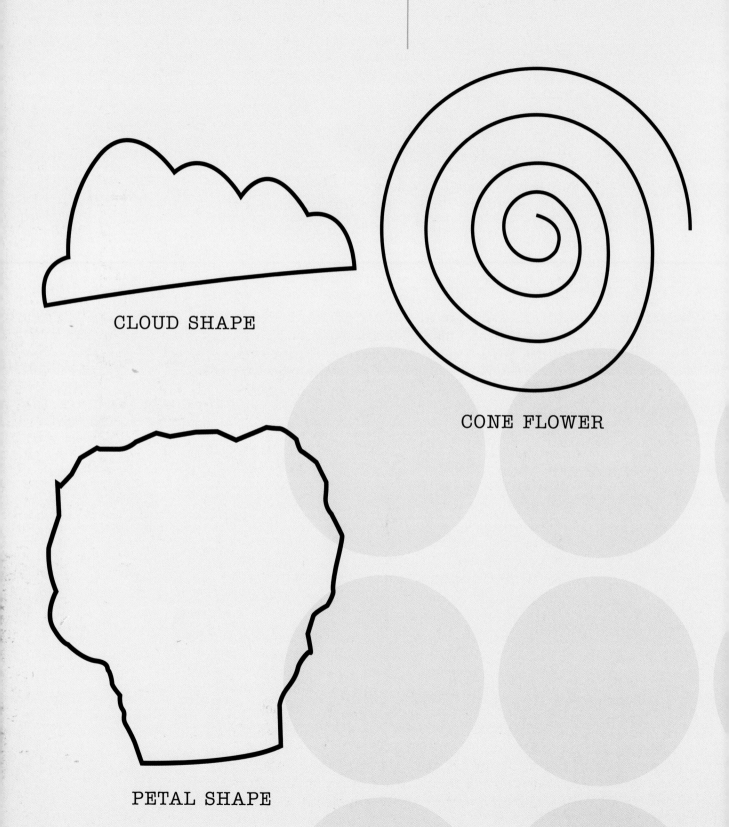

CLOUD SHAPE

CONE FLOWER

PETAL SHAPE

# more about Ronda and her dorkapolis world

Hello everyone! My name is Ronda, like the Beach Boy's song, "Help me Rhonda," only no "h" (which I have been saying my whole life). I currently live in the suburbs of Denver, Colorado, with my husband Andy and two amazing teens, Lexi and Anthony. My house is ruled by three adorable Chihuahuas: Nina, Pedro and Chloe. I love being a work-at-home mom and I love all things crafty: scrapping, cooking, knitting, sewing, reading and photography. I love traveling with my family and hope to explore more of this great big world of ours. You can usually find me in my craft room creating with music blaring in the background, or in the kitchen baking for my kids. I have been into art since I was a kid and have always loved it. In high school, I was editor of my high school paper and layouts were my specialty. I loved piecing together everything that had to go on the page and making sense of it all. So when my daughter came along, scrapbooking seemed to be the next natural step. I got to play with paper, write stories and capture memories. I love that scrapbooking allows me to incorporate all my artistic loves, be it messy or just working with my photography. Some of my proudest scrapbook moments are being named a Memory Makers Master in 2009, starting the One Little Word Scrapbook challenge blog and being a team member for many great manufacturing design teams, including the Cocoa Daisy design team. I have also been blessed with being published in books and magazines: **Memory Makers**, **Scrapbook Trends**, **Creating Keepsakes** and **Artful Blogging**, as well as in some great idea books. I like to call my style "Uptown Antique Brie"—a little class, a little vintage and a lot of good cheese. I love the new, flashy stuff, but have an appreciation for vintage items. I love to push the envelope and use products in unconventional ways, and I love using bold colors and combining colors in ways that surprise people. Most of my layouts—if not all—are cheesy; emotions and everyday moments are among my favorite subjects to scrap.

# resources

The following companies manufacture products featured in this book. Please check your local retailers to find these materials, or go to the companies' websites for the latest products. In addition, we have made every attempt to properly credit the items mentioned in this book. We apologize to any company that we have listed incorrectly, and we would appreciate hearing from you.

**3ndy Papir Co**
www.3ndypapir.no

**7 Gypsies**
www.sevengypsies.com

**American Crafts, Inc.**
www.americancrafts.com

**Amy Butler**
www.amybutlerdesign.com

**BasicGrey, LLC.**
www.basicgrey.com

**Bazzill Basics Paper**
www.bazzillbasics.com

**Butterick**
www.butterick.mccall.com

**Canvas Corp**
www.canvascorp.com

**Cocoa Daisy**
www.cocoadaisy.com

**Collage Press**
www.collagepress.com

**Cosmo Cricket**
www.cosmocricket.com

**Crafter's Workshop, The**
www.thecraftersworkshop.com

**Crate Paper, Inc.**
www.cratepaper.com

**Designer Digitals**
www.designerdigitals.com

**DMC**
www.dmc-usa.com

**Doodlebug Design Inc.**
www.doodlebug.ws

**Echo Park Paper Co.**
www.echoparkpaper.com

**EK Success**
www.eksuccessbrands.com

**Etsy Inc., Kenner Road**
www.etsy.com/shop/kennerroad

**Etsy Inc., Living Room Floor**
www.etsy.com/shop/livingroomfloor

**Etsy Inc., Mothball Charlie**
www.etsy.com/shop/mothballcharlie

**Fancy Pants Design**
www.fancypantsdesigns.com

**Fiskars**
www.fiskars.com

**Girls' Paperie, The**
www.thegirlspaperie.com

**Glitz Design, LLC**
www.glitzitnow.com

**Golden Artist Colors, Inc.**
www.goldenpaints.com

**Graphic 45**
www.g45papers.com

**Hambly Screenprints**
www.hamblyscreenprints.com

**Helmar USA, Inc.**
www.helmarusa.com

**J&P Coats**
www.coatsandclark.com

**Jenni Bowlin**
www.jbsmercantile.com

**Jillibean Soup**
www.jillibean-soup.com

**K&Company**
www.eksuccessbrands.com/kandcompany

**Kaisercraft**
www.kaisercraft.net

**KI Memories Inc.**
www.kimemories.com

**Lily Bee Design**
www.lilybeedesign.com

**Liquitex**
www.liquitex.com

**Little Yellow Bicycle**
www.mylyb.com

**Making Memories**
www.makingmemories.com

**Martha Stewart Crafts**
www.marthastewartcrafts.eksuccessbrands.com

**May Arts**
www.mayarts.com

**Maya Road, LLC**
www.mayaroad.net

**Me & My Big Ideas**
www.meandmybigideas.com

**My Mind's Eye**
www.mymindseye.com

**October Afternoon**
www.octoberafternoon.com

**Papier Valise**
www.papiervalise.com

**Petaloo**
www.petaloo.cameoez.com/Scripts/PublicSite

**Pink Paislee**
www.pinkpaislee.com

**Prima Marketing Inc.**
www.primamarketing.com

**Purple Onion Designs**
www.purpleoniondesigns.com

**Ranger Industries, Inc.**
www.rangerink.com

**Sakura Color Products of America, Inc.**
www.sakuraofamerica.com

**Sassafras Lass**
www.sassafraslass.com

**Shimmerz Paints**
www.shimmerzpaints.com

**Stampin' Up**
www.stampinup.com

**Strano Designs Inc.**
www.stranodesigns.com

**Strathmore**
www.strathmoreartist.com

**Studio Calico**
www.studiocalico.com

**Tattered Angels**
www.mytatteredangels.com

**Teresa Collins Designs**
www.teresacollinsdesigns.com

**Tim Holtz**
www.timholtz.com

**Tsukineko, LLC**
www.tsukineko.com

**Twinery, The**
www.thetwinery.com

**Wendy Vecchi Studio 490/Stampers Anonymous**
www.stampersanonymous.com

**Wilton Industries**
www.wilton.com

# index

## acknowledgments

Thank you to some very special friends.

I couldn't have done this book without the incredible support of F+W Media, North Light Books. So many talented hands made this book come to life and I am proud to be an author with such a fantastic company. Huge thanks to this amazing team.

Thank you to Christine Doyle. I like the second e-mail the best! Your quick response and hard work brought my book to life and I am so appreciative. Thank you.

Thank you to the most awesome wicked editor, Bethany Anderson. You are EPIC and the perfect pairing for me. You get me. You really get me and have made this journey incredibly fun. I love how you pushed and pulled me in all the right ways to bring out the best in me. My favorite moments are you telling me to chill and grab a Chai. I am forever thankful for all of your hard work and dedication.

Thank you to my fabulous photographer, Christine Polomsky. It was a pleasure to spend a week with you while you photographed the techniques. I am still laughing at our good times. You brought my creations to life in such an awesome way. Thank you.

Thank you to Kelly O'Dell for creating a stunning backdrop, and a beautiful cover and interior for my book. You amaze me with your talent and I am forever grateful for all that you have done.

Thank you to Ric Deliantoni for keeping me calm during the video shoots, and making me feel normal and like a rock star at the same time. I truly appreciate it.

Lisa, you rock my world—you gave me wings to fly and held my hand along the way. You were always there for me, encouraging me, kicking me into gear, laughing with me and, best of all, just being my friend throughout this process. You were there at the creation of this idea, prodding me to chase down my dream. I am forever grateful for all the advice and love you showered me with over the last year.

Christine, I was blessed to also have your encouragement and support throughout this process. Thank you for letting me hash out ideas with you on the long plane ride home and for letting me go into "book mode" without worries. You are beautiful, my friend.

Ali, I am so honored to call you "friend." Your words at breakfast one day spurred me into action and made me believe in myself. Funny how the words "Oh, you should so do it" can be so uplifting. Thank you from the bottom of my heart.

Martha, Emily and Jessi, thank you for always being there for me and supporting me no matter what. You always know what I need even when I don't. You allow me to be myself without worries, which is so phenomenal. I love you all.

Steph and Nicky, you gave me hope when I needed it the most. Your words reaching out to me when I thought all was lost kept me going. I keep those words close to my heart.

Special thanks to Kristen at Lily Bee Designs and Gudrun at 3ndy Papir for allowing me to turn their beautiful papers into paper lace for my cover.

Special thanks to Tracy and Helmar USA for generously donating all the adhesives I used on the projects in the book.

Thank you to all the fabulous companies who very generously donated their products: 3ndy Papir Co., Cocoa Daisy, Cosmo Cricket, Crate Paper, Hambly Studios, Helmar Adhesives, Jenni Bowlin Studio, Lily Bee Designs, Maya Road, October Afternoon, Pink Paislee, Purple Onion Designs, Ranger Industries, Studio Calico, Studio 490/Stampers Anonymous, The Crafter's Workshop and The Girls' Paperie.

16   15   14   13   12     5   4   3   2   1

Distributed in Canada by Fraser Direct
100 Armstrong Avenue
Georgetown, ON, Canada  L7G 5S4
Tel: (905) 877-4411

Distributed in the U.K. and Europe by F&W MEDIA INTERNATIONAL
Brunel House, Newton Abbot, Devon, TQ12 4PU, England
Tel: (+44) 1626 323200, Fax: (+44) 1626 323319
Email: enquiries@fwmedia.com

Distributed in Australia by Capricorn Link
P.O. Box 704, S. Windsor NSW, 2756 Australia
Tel: (02) 4577-3555

**fw**
*media*
www.fwmedia.com

SRN: W1820
ISBN-13: 978-1-59963-284-1
ISBN-10: 1-59963-284-5

Edited by **Bethany Anderson**

Designed by **Kelly O'Dell**

Production coordinated by **Greg Nock**

Photography by **Christine Polomsky**
and **Ric Deliantoni**

Photo-styling by **Lauren Emmerling**

Studio shots provided by **Ronda Palazzari**

## metric conversion chart

| to convert | to | multiply by |
| --- | --- | --- |
| Inches | Centimeters | 2.54 |
| Centimeters | Inches | 0.4 |
| Feet | Centimeters | 30.5 |
| Centimeters | Feet | 0.03 |
| Yards | Meters | 0.9 |
| Meters | Yards | 1.1 |

# 50 techniques not enough? We have plenty more to offer!

Ronda Palazzari has taught you how to flick, splatter and mist your way through **Art of Layers** and still has more to offer. In these two free downloads you'll learn the most basic and surprising way to make a text-filled background with paint, plus learn the coolest way to drip paint to add a touch of texture and color to any craft.

Get two free bonus techniques, Painted Stamps and Drips of Paint, online at: http://www.createmixedmedia.com/layers-bonus.

**CREATIVE FOUNDATIONS**
Offering simple techniques with stunning results using common supplies, giving plenty of ideas with a variety of projects.

A Great Community to Inspire You Every Day!
**CreateMixedMedia.com**
**ShopMixedMedia.com**

For exclusive free projects, tutorials and e-books, blogs, podcasts, reviews, special offers and more!

For inspiration delivered to your inbox, sign up for our free e-mail newsletter.

Or join the fun at:

 **Facebook.com/CreateMixedMedia.com**

 **@cMixedMedia**

**DELIGHT IN THE SEASONS**
For any season, and any event, the projects will add sparkle and warmth to any papercraft or craft project.

**NORTH LIGHT BOOKS**